ðOOðLE
INTERPRETATION
 a beginner's guide

MICHAEL WATTS

Hodder & Stoughton
A MEMBER OF THE HODDER HEADLINE GROUP

Acknowledgments

Grateful thanks to Bella magazine for regularly featuring my doodle analyses, and for their foreword to this book. To Robert Lortscher and to many of my clients who inspired me with their creative doodling. Finally special thanks to my parents for all their support and to my wife Iwona for her constant encouragement and advice.

Orders: please contact Bookpoint Ltd, 39 Milton Park, Abingdon, Oxon OX14 4TD. Telephone: (44) 01235 400414, Fax: (44) 01235 400454. Lines are open from 9.00–6.00, Monday to Saturday, with a 24-hour message answering service. Email address: orders@bookpoint.co.uk

British Library Cataloguing in Publication Data
A catalogue record for this title is available from The British Library

ISBN 0 340 77251 4

First published 2000
Impression number 10 9 8 7 6 5 4 3 2 1
Year   2005 2004 2003 2002 2001 2000

Copyright © 2000 Michael Watts

Typeset by Transet Limited, Coventry, England.
Printed in Great Britain for Hodder & Stoughton Educational, a division of Hodder Headline plc, 338 Euston Road, London NW1 3BH by Cox and Wyman Limited, Reading, Berks.

CONTENTS

Chapter 1   What exactly are doodles? 1

Why do we doodle?   1
The historical background of doodle interpretation   2
The basis of doodle interpretation   3
About this book   4

Chapter 2   Where to begin?   5

Getting your doodle samples   5
What about non-doodlers?   6
Do I need any background information on the doodler?   6
Is there anything else I need?   7
Practice   7

**Chapter 3   If you doodled a tree,
how would it be?   8**

Trees – their place in mythology   8
The interpretation of tree doodles   9
Tree characteristics   13
Practice   15

Chapter 4   Complex doodles   16

What is a complex doodle?   16
Hearts   16
Faces   18
Human figures   29

Penises	32
Snakes	33
Houses	35
Numbers	38
Arrows	39
Practice	40

Chapter 5 A helping hand to interpret doodles 41

The role of intuition and logic in doodle interpretation	41
What is the difference between someone's regular doodles, and those they rarely produce?	42
How to spot romantic doodles	42
Detecting sexual doodles	42
Conflicting meanings in doodles	43
Interpreting ink colour	43
The significance of positioning	45
Various drawing styles that can add to the symbolic interpretation of doodles	48
Practice	52

Chapter 6 Abstract/geometric doodles 53

The significance of abstract and geometric doodles	53
Lines	53
Loops	55
Repetitive patterns	56
Three-dimensional forms	57
Geometric forms	58
Abstract doodles	65
Practice	68

Chapter 7 Animal/insect doodles 69

The significance of animal doodles	69
Interpretation of animal doodles	69

The significance of insect doodles 79
Interpretation of insect doodles 79

Chapter 8   The A–Z of doodles   82

Practice 111

Chapter 9   Therapeutic doodles   112

What are therapeutic doodles? 112
Why is doodle therapy effective? 113
When to do the exercises 113
Some helpful tips 114
How long will it take to experience the benefits? 114
Doodle therapy exercises 115
Melting anger/creating humour/dissolving stress 115
Enhancing physical co-ordination 117
Improving mental focus and motivation 118

Index   121

FOREWORD

Michael Watts contributed a highly successful doodle analysis column to *Bella*. Many readers and members of staff who had doodles interpreted were amazed by his uncanny accuracy. Now, with this extremely well written book, you will be able to instantly interpret any doodle you are likely to come across. We recommend it to everybody and know that you will find it enjoyable, invaluable and easy to use.

Bella

WhAT EXACTly ARE OOOOLES?

In some dictionaries, doodles are defined as being 'diagrams of the subconscious' – an apt description, because they are one of the many subtle voices that this part of our mind uses for self-expression. Consequently, psychiatrists and psychoanalysts often use doodle interpretation as an aid to assessing personality. Doodles come in all shapes and sizes, appearing on telephone pads, magazines, shopping lists, work notes etc., and they are usually produced in a semi-automatic manner, whilst our mind is in a preoccupied or trance-like state of consciousness. Beneath the surface appearance of many a doodle, lies an intimate story of the owner's hidden emotions, secret desires, fantasies, fears and phobias. These revealing pictures are symbolic transmissions from the deepest levels of our being. The secretary or PA on the telephone, a typist's shorthand pad, a business executive at a boardroom meeting – all reveal hidden aspects of their personality whilst they innocently doodle on paper in front of them.

Why oo we ooooLe?

Almost everyone doodles, either occasionally or on a regular basis – for some individuals it's even an addiction. The widespread popularity of this habit is evident in the fortune spent each year removing, from numerous public places, doodles drawn in pen, pencil, lipstick and paint.

Even if you just underline things or add decorative frills to certain letters in your own name you are still doodling, and this activity is not, as some people choose to believe, simply the meaningless product of a bored or preoccupied mind.

When someone has an extremely important decision to make, or a difficult problem to solve, the action of doodling helps to siphon off excessive tension and anxiety and prevent the intrusion of unwanted thoughts that distract. Doodling also serves as an escape valve for restrained feelings of frustration, anger or impatience, and for blocked emotions brewing in our subconscious.

Similar to the chant of a mantra, the repetition of lines and shapes typical of doodling helps us to relax and collect our thoughts, so our thinking processes become clearer and more effective. We can then concentrate more efficiently and, whilst the main beam of our attention is involved in some other activity, pent-up as well as repressed emotions can be 'doodled away' safely, without any disturbance to our conscious mind.

In addition, aesthetically constructed complex abstract patterns or other impressively drawn doodles frequently signify unexpressed artistic potential.

The historical background of doodle interpretation

Awareness of the potentially symbolic significance of pictures or shapes is nothing new. For thousands of years civilizations have consciously used symbolic imagery in their drawings to depict their innermost thoughts and feelings – Egyptian hieroglyphics are perhaps one of the earliest examples of this practice.

Since the birth of modern-day psychology, the interpretation of doodle symbolism has been one of many methods used to probe the depths of the subconscious mind. This is primarily thanks to the work of Sigmund Freud and Carl Jung – the two great 'fathers' of twentieth-century psychology. They realized that this deeper part of our being communicates its nature surreptitiously, via a coded language of symbols, images and gestures rather than words, and that by examining and interpreting this secret code we can reach a fuller understanding of who we are.

As a result of these profound insights, psychologists, psychiatrists and others in the field of personality assessment now devote considerable time to uncovering the clandestine meaning of the symbols and gestures of various important facets of human expression, including dreams, body gestures and (last, but not least) doodling.

Freud and Jung's research into the symbolic significance of doodles and drawings spawned a new branch of psychology known as **analytical drawing psychology**, in which the creative features, figures and formations of a person's artwork are analysed to reveal the feelings that lie beneath the surface.

The Basis of Doodle Interpretation

Sigmund Freud believed that the pictures or patterns we make in the process of doodling are sometimes a disguised or symbolic expression of repressed sexual traumas, hidden sexual desires or hostile feelings which we find too shameful or disturbing to consciously acknowledge. He noticed that we use the defence mechanism of 'censorship' to repress these unwanted parts of our psyche so that we are able to escape conscious feelings of guilt or inadequacy and maintain an outer appearance of equilibrium. This repression causes a build-up of internal tension. Freud felt that doodles (and dreams) act as escape valves by allowing the mind to express these 'improper' thoughts and impulses in a covert and acceptable manner. This provides some sort of release for blocked emotional and sexual energy, festering in our subconscious, which would otherwise remain unexpressed.

Carl Jung also accepted that doodles and drawings symbolically express subconscious thoughts and feelings, but he was more interested in their therapeutic benefits. He observed, in particular, the calming effect experienced by certain patients whilst they doodled circles with shapes inside (mandalas).

About this book

This book is the product of my 18 years' experience as a psychologist and handwriting expert, during which time I have analysed hundreds of doodles. The high degree of accuracy in this book has been greatly helped by the feedback I have received from this work.

Many of the principles here have been gleaned from my experience in analytical drawing psychology. Popularly called **art therapy**, this reliable body of knowledge – derived from projective drawing tests and psychiatric findings – offers much insight into the psyche via an interpretation of an individual's artwork and other creative expressions, including doodles.

I have also applied classic graphological principles to the interpretation of lines and shapes used in the formation of each doodle. Finally, many of the translations of symbolic imagery come from the research of Jung and Freud.

What subconscious desires are you carrying around with you right now, and how should you deal with them? Are you feeling uptight at this moment but don't know why? Would you like to know more about your friends, relatives, people you work with – or perhaps your lover? A glance at what's been doodled might hold the answers you're looking for. The contents section or alternatively the alphabetically ordered list of doodles in the index of this book, will direct you to the relevant page where you can look up the meaning of your doodle.

*A*re you a complete novice to doodle interpretation? If so, this may be your last chance to get a relatively unbiased sample of your own doodles – assuming you don't have this already. So keep within easy reach a blank sheet of paper and suitable pen. Then wait for, or create, the sort of situation where you are most likely to doodle and just let your pen take over – many people find that their favourite time for doodling is when they are occupied on the telephone. It would be great if you can also get some samples from friends, family or work colleagues. You'll find it fascinating referring to these and your own doodles as you travel through the informative pages of this book.

GETTING YOUR DOODLE SAMPLES

The ideal samples for interpretation are those that have been produced naturally and spontaneously – with a pen, and ink colour, of the writer's choice – rather than intentionally provided for analysis. If possible, ask the person to point out which doodles he or she frequently draws, and which are rare. If you cannot get hold of such examples use the following procedure.

If possible, the samples should be drawn on a blank sheet of A4 paper in the type of pen/ink colour the person normally uses. The samples should include, and indicate, doodles that form a regular part of the writer's repertoire (these reveal the more dominant aspects of personality) as well as those that feature only rarely.

You can, if you wish, simply get someone to create doodles for you on the spot – as naturally as they can. It is better, however, to ask them to provide you with a sample they produced under the sort of circumstances in which they might have doodled anyway – this way it will be less contrived.

What about non-doodlers?

If a person insists they never doodle, you can still find out a lot about them by getting them to draw a tree. Chapter 3 interprets these in detail. Trees are highly revealing **complex doodles** (doodles that have a wide range of potential symbolic meanings depending on their style). Houses and faces, also in this category, can be used for the same purpose – see Chapter 4. Even if you have already compiled a personality profile from your own or someone else's habitual doodles, you can gain further insights from drawings of trees, houses or faces.

Do I need any background information on the doodler?

Not necessarily, but without it there is the risk of occasionally making some major errors in interpretation. Ideally, therefore, you should find out if the doodler is male or female, adult or child. It is also good to know their approximate age. This sort of information can be very helpful to you. For instance, if an adult's doodle has a very immature appearance, then in addition to the various other characteristics revealed by the doodle you will also be able to deduce a childlike side to their nature which is bound to influence their behaviour.

There are women who produce doodles that are typically masculine, and some men doodle patterns and pictures that are very feminine. Knowing someone's sex will sometimes give you a good indication as to the proportion or balance of female and male characteristics in their personality.

Finally, shakiness or wobbly line formation in a doodle from someone very old is not unusual, whereas the same characteristic in a much younger person could point to severe anxiety, or health problems.

Is there anything else I need?

It is a good idea to keep a file with samples of all the doodles you have analysed. This should include your interpretations and, wherever possible, the person's response to your analysis. Positive reactions will increase your confidence and you will learn from your mistakes by noting down any negative reactions.

Practice on family and friends first, so that you build up some experience before testing your skills on strangers.

PRACTICE

Why is it important to distinguish between doodles someone regularly produces and doodles that they produce only rarely? (A full answer to this question can be found in Chapter 5.)

3 IF YOU DOODLED A TREE, HOW WOULD IT BE?

Since ancient times, the tree has always symbolized life, the potential for expansion on all levels of being – physical, emotional and spiritual. Fed by water (emotion) it grows towards the sky (spiritual) and out of the dead earth (nothingness). It symbolizes fulfilling one's destiny by surrendering to inner forces of growth and the guidance that comes from the unconscious. In the same way that trees reach great heights only if they are firmly rooted in the earth, human consciousness can only fully develop if it has total support from the unconscious mind.

TREES – THEIR PLACE IN MYTHOLOGY

In mythology, the growing tree has long been considered a symbol of immortality; the apple of the knowledge of good and evil was picked from a tree in the paradisiacal Garden of Eden. The Kabbalistic Tree of Life is a diagram of the creation of the infinite universe and the human psyche. Chinese, Japanese, Hindu and Sumerian mythology all have heavens in which sacred trees bear fine fruit. The Australian aborigines believe that The Great Tree supports the heavens themselves, and in many societies, the action of climbing a tree symbolizes progress towards paradise.

Trees have clearly occupied a prominent position in humanity's collective unconscious, which seems to explain the exceptionally revealing nature of tree doodles. This realization has inspired many psychologists to use tree analysis in their work. So why not doodle a tree right now (or get someone else to do so), and then look up the meaning in the following sections.

The INTERPRETATION OF TREE DOODLES

Tree with rounded, cloud-shaped crown

This sociable, kind-hearted, affectionate character is a good listener and a fluent talker. Their resourceful imagination, initiative and knack for finding short cuts will help them find success in most careers that depend on good communication skills. They have a healthy sexual appetite and their lovemaking is sensual and uninhibited.

Tree with completely bare branches

Indicates a tense person who can be sarcastic and judgemental towards partners. They bottle up emotions and can't relax. Ambitious and efficient, they best suit jobs requiring minimum social contact as they lack diplomacy and patience, and dislike dealing with authority. In lovemaking this character is unlikely to be considerate, as sex for them is merely a stress release.

Tree with leaves and fruit

An open-minded, hospitable individual who loves all the sensual pleasures of life. Ideally suited to careers requiring imagination, progressive thinking, verbal fluency and good social skills. Emotionally mature and affectionate, this person is a romantic lover with a good sense of humour. Considerate, they will devote plenty of time to the sensuous delights of foreplay.

Tree with a messy, haphazard appearance

This overworked, frustrated adrenaline addict is insecure because of an over-demanding ego that is never satisfied. Fast thinking, with an incisive, creative mind, they are bound to succeed. Unfortunately, low self-esteem and fears from a difficult childhood have made them anxious about the future. Impulsive, they take on far too much, which makes them tense, impatient and easily provoked to anger. They lack sensitivity and emotional maturity, so their partners will often feel neglected and unloved.

Christmas tree with triangular-shaped branches

This energetic, unconventional person has a natural fighting spirit, strong principles, an affinity with nature and a love of the outdoor life. Intelligent, goal-orientated, self-disciplined and persistent, they will work hard to achieve a solid foundation to their life. Being highly assertive, they detest following orders and will want a position of authority or independence in their career. In a relationship they are intolerant, critical, uncompromising and domineering. When stressed they will be fussy and argumentative. This person has abundant sexual stamina but lacks sensitivity, so lovemaking is very predictable.

Weeping willow or any other tree with sagging or arched branches

This suggests loneliness, sadness and regret due to domestic or job-related problems. This person's pessimism wears them out – they are withdrawn and secretive, hiding their thoughts and feelings even from their closest friends. They need ego boosting and reassurance to allay fears that are the product of deep emotional insecurity. When they lose control, their temper is explosive. When things go wrong they become terribly moody and depressed.

Tree with branches that are formed with broken lines

This person's difficult childhood has made them neurotic. Impulsive, they plunge into relationships and make decisions without much thought. They have a vivid, creative imagination, a sharp analytical mind and plenty of stamina – they should do well in their career.

High adrenaline levels make them sexually demanding. They should give up coffee and other stimulants, and exercise more, to overcome their insomnia and stress.

A WITHERED TREE

Symbolizes the dried-up state of someone who lives too much in the head. Doctrines and rules have taken the place of natural instinct, intuition, compassion and sensuality. This person feels a sense of emptiness and guilt.

BRANCHES REACHING UPWARDS

Reveals an opportunist and daydreamer who looks on the bright side of life – they recover quickly from any setbacks. They are completely absorbed by stimulating projects and their ambition, determination and self-assurance will ensure success. Their enthusiastic manner provides charisma and helps them make friends, and a natural *joie de vivre* enhances their relationships.

TWO TREES SLANTING IN OPPOSITE DIRECTIONS

Indicates a dual emotional nature – one side sociable, warm and affectionate, the other, reserved, cold and uninterested. This person is often overcontrolled as their intellect is constantly trying to rule their feelings and impulses. They find it difficult to stick to routine and suffer from indecision.

PALM TREE

Reveals a powerful desire to escape from the daily duties and worries of existence to a trouble-free life of leisure and pleasure.

Tree characteristics

If any of the following tree characteristics are applicable, then add their corresponding meanings to your tree personality profile.

Tree that is shaded, creating a very dark appearance

Shading any type of tree will reduce its positive interpretations and intensify its negative interpretations. Shading suggests a person who focuses on the negative, darker aspects of existence, and this causes them to alternate between anger and depression. They feel anxious and discouraged and in a self-questioning state of mind. This may stem from job-related failures or a troubled love life – perhaps a recent break-up.

TREE ON AN ISLAND

Indicates a strong desire to increase economic and emotional security. Frightened of loneliness, but on guard with strangers, this individual doesn't make friends easily. They value old friendships and family, and will be monogamous in a relationship with someone they love.

TREE ON A HILLSIDE

Reveals caution and a dislike of casual socializing. This person sticks to one or two old friendships, and is loyal in intimate relationships but emotionally suppressed. They like to work independently, and are ambitious and optimistic about the future.

TREE WITH LONG ROOTS

Being practical minded and realistic, this person doesn't expect any free rides. They strongly value material security and their determination and natural fighting spirit sees them through the inevitable ups and downs. Though constantly on the move and productive, they still have enough energy to maintain a healthy sex life. A good balance between head and heart.

TREE WITH A KNOT IN THE TRUNK

Reveals an inability to forget traumatic childhood experiences. The emotional scars have created a grudge-bearing nature that makes them prone to sulking.

TREE WITH A WIDE BASE AND THICK TRUNK

This person possesses the self-assurance, stamina and motivation to create a secure base in their career, social life and intimate relationships. Down-to-earth, emotionally balanced and friendly, they communicate well and make friends easily. Their sexual appetite is strong but they are interested only in serious long-term relationships – definitely not the type for one-night stands.

TREE WITH LONG THIN TRUNK

Ruled by the intellect and ego rather than the heart, this person thinks too much, which prevents them from experiencing life through the body and senses. An activity like chi kung or t'ai chi is what they need to become physically and mentally more balanced.

TREE THAT HAS BEEN FELLED OR UPROOTED

The masculine and feminine elements of this personality are not in harmony and this is causing an identity crisis. Guilt or other unhealthy emotions from childhood have made them uneasy with their sexuality.

PRACTICE

1 Using the information in this chapter, compose your own personality profile from a doodle of a tree with leaves and fruit that has been darkly shaded.
2 Practice drawing trees that have an extremely messy, haphazard appearance. Try to tune into the state of mind of someone who doodles this type of tree, by closely observing how you feel physically and emotionally during the action of doodling the tree. This will enhance your interpretation skills at a kinaesthetic level.

COMPLEX DOODLES

Doodles do not need to closely resemble the example provided for the interpretation to apply.

What is a complex doodle?

Doodles are called 'complex doodles' if they have a very wide range of potentially different meanings that are influenced by the style in which they are drawn. Some complex doodles can be used as a specific exercise to derive additional information about someone after you have analysed their habitual doodles. Houses and faces can be used for this purpose, as well as trees (see Chapter 3).

Hearts

Long before its physiological role was recognized, the heart was regarded as the very root of life itself. It has always held the supreme place among the organs of the body as the symbol of our being, the centre of our emotional lives – the seat of our thoughts and feelings, of love, courage and the conscience. Its symbolic nature is evident in doodles of hearts by people in love and in linguistic expressions such as 'broken heart'. The rejected partner in a broken relationship also sometimes produces heart doodles.

People who draw hearts invariably have a compassionate side that is capable of deep empathy for another person's problems. There is also a very childlike, innocent aspect to their nature – their emotional behaviour and approach to love and relationships is often reminiscent of a young adolescent.

Dearts that are gently curved at the base

Indicate a compassionate, warm and romantic sexual nature, possessing loyalty and a high regard for fidelity.

Dearts that are sharply pointed at the base

Reveals a highly judgemental person with a jealous streak – the qualities associated with curved hearts will be instantly switched off if a mate does not conform closely to their standards, especially in lovemaking. For this type, there is no romance without sex.

Dearts with an arrow through them

Discloses a childish, romantic and compulsive daydreamer, who is in love with love. When involved in an intimate relationship, this doodler will be jealous and possessive and prepared to fight to regain a lost love. This doodle frequently indicates unrequited love and sexual passion. A sharply pointed tip on the arrow will indicate mixed emotions of anger, jealousy and depression; a rounded arrow tip will disclose sadness and regret but no aggresive feelings.

HEARTS DIVIDED INTO TWO OR MORE PIECES

This reveals severe depression due to a broken or unhappy relationship.

TWO OVERLAPPING HEARTS

A sure sign of a harmonious, loving relationship.

HEARTS INSIDE HEARTS

Reveals a romantic who finds it difficult to let someone they love know about it. In relationships these people can become extremely possessive and their love tends to inhibit their partner's freedom and personal growth.

A HEART INSIDE A CIRCLE

A sign of deep loneliness.

A HEAVILY SHADED-IN OR BLACK HEART

Shows deep depression stemming from long-term emotional isolation or a recently ended relationship.

FACES

Human facial expressions can reveal a great deal about a person's thoughts and feelings. The expression you see on a doodled face often closely mirrors a person's actual mental and emotional state of mind.

FACIAL PROFILES

FACE PROFILE LOOKING TO THE RIGHT

Reveals someone who escapes from unpleasant memories by focusing enthusiastically on ambitious plans for the future. This friendly, open personality feels at ease in social settings and enjoys the companionship of others.

facial profile looking to the left

This suggests an introspective, socially reserved, private nature that is often hidden behind a mask of self-assurance. These types are prisoners of the unhappiness they felt earlier in life, and they cling to the security of what is routine and familiar. No matter how much they achieve, they are inwardly self-critical.

facial profiles looking both ways

A sign of very changeable moods and social attitudes – sometimes outgoing, friendly and affectionate, at other times shy, mistrustful and detached, with a need for complete privacy and solitude. Also reveals ambivalent feelings towards parents – loyalties shifting from one to the other.

facial types

Completed face

Indicates a sociable personality with extrovert tendencies. This person needs a career and a social life that provides plenty of contact with others.

Unhappy face

People around this person are not being pleasant. This face clearly reveals someone who is going through a stressful, unhappy period because of job-related problems, or emotional and sexual frustration stemming from a troubled relationship. This person is feeling unhappy and pessimistic.

Happy or smiling face

Shows a sense of humour and fun. This individual strives hard to avoid the hardships of existence and enjoy family and friends. They seem sexually content.

Beautiful face

A sign of love and compassion for human beings – a focusing on the positive qualities of people and situations. This optimistic, good-natured individual thoroughly enjoys social activities.

Ugly or angry face

Currently this person lacks *joie de vivre* because their confidence is suffering and they feel annoyed at themselves as well as bitter and resentful towards certain people in their life who have hurt them.

Shocked-looking face

This person is troubled by unhappy traumatic events.

Cruel or domineering face

Signifies resentment of authority figures and a desire for increased personal power.

Size of face

A very large face indicates a forceful, confident ego with an active intellect and vivid fantasy. A very small face discloses someone who feels physically, socially or intellectually inferior.

Very round face

Shows a basically kind nature. Someone who loves food.

Heavily shaded face

Reveals an emotional, passionate nature with perceptiveness and good intuition. At the moment certain problems are making this person feel anxious, tense, irritable and depressed, and they have entered a self-questioning state of mind. This person likes people but also needs privacy, and fears being imposed upon. If the shaded face is of the opposite sex, then this indicates mixed feelings of anger and love towards a lover, due to a recent break-up, or because of sexual and emotional disharmony in the relationship.

Odd faces with fantasy features

A sense of fun and an off-beat sense of humour is revealed in really weirdly shaped ears, eyes or other features – including ones that do not exist in reality. This person is independent minded and has a vivid, creative imagination.

Facial features

No facial features

Figures with no facial features show a disturbed state of mind and reveal depression and social isolation – a sense of feeling lonely and unable to connect with others.

Eyes

Eye doodles reflect several potential meanings. They may symbolize a capacity for wisdom, self-knowledge and perceptiveness that is currently being ignored. They frequently represent the discriminating, all-seeing eye of the person's higher consciousness that is acting as an internal censor, constantly passing judgement on their thoughts, feelings and behaviour. In someone with spiritual aspirations this doodle can be a symbol of their true self, which is calling out for their attention. It also often reflects a person's attitude to life and other people. Are the eyes sad, angry or frightened? The emotion you see in the eye mirrors the emotional state of the doodler.

Large eyes indicate someone who is mistrustful, observant, with a sensitive nature that is easily hurt by criticism.

Very small or closed eyes are a sign of sadness, emotional withdrawal and repressed anger.

Pupils omitted demonstrate a shallow, unevolved attitude to existence.

Eyes with a mischievous glint show a bizarre sense of humour and excellent powers of observation.

Upward-slanting eyes indicate an alert, perceptive person with psychic sensitivity and a strong survival streak. They won't be pushed around or taken advantage of.

Eyes that are cross-eyed show a sense of humour that masks a fearful attitude to life.

Third eye on face

The **third eye** – or Ajna chakra, as it is called in yoga – is likely to be a subconscious signal to this person that they should listen more closely to their inner guru, the source of heightened awareness and psychic or spiritual strength inside each person. This  doodle reveals an interest in occultism and a genuine desire to reach a higher level of consciousness.

Eyebrows

Very thin eyebrows indicate a well-groomed, self-conscious, fussy and vain person.

Very thick, low, bushy brows are drawn by a forceful, frustrated, angry person.

Raised eyebrows indicate a desire to control and a streak of cynicism.

Eyelashes

A female doodler of eyelashes is very fashion conscious and vain. She thoroughly enjoys flirting, but has strong feelings of apprehension towards going any further. A mistrust of people prevents her from letting go sexually. A male doodler of eyelashes has strong femininity in his personality. He is vain, narcissistic, and may be repressing bisexual tendencies.

Nose

In ancient folklore the size of the nose was believed to correlate with genital size, and there is a close connection between the nose and the sexual reflexes. Swelling of the nasal spongy tissues and congestion of the nose occur during sexual excitement, and there is known to be a direct connection between sneezing and orgasm. It is not surprising that nose doodles are primarily symbolic of sexual attitudes and behaviour.

Faces drawn without a nose reveal a childish streak, an emotionally dependent nature and sexual immaturity.

Noses by female doodlers

Noses that are very small, or sharply pointed, or drooping noticeably downwards indicate a strong dissatisfaction with a lover's sexual performance. These doodles also suggest hostility towards men in general.

Noses with a rounded tip that points horizontally or upwards suggest fond feelings towards a partner and a light-hearted, open attitude towards sex. If the nose is also extremely large, this may reveal a strong fascination for the male anatomy, and a huge sexual appetite.

Noses by male doodlers

A small nose indicates fear of impotence and a complex about genital size.

A large nose suggests a large sexual appetite and genital self-confidence.

Mouth (Lips/Tongue)

Symbolic of the lips of the vagina, the mouth often reveals sexual and social behaviour patterns.

Full, fleshy lips indicate a very sensual lover who especially enjoys passionate kissing and oral sex.

Parted lips are a sign of someone who is on the lookout for a satisfying relationship. This person likes flirting and is skilful in erotic, seductive conversation.

Parted lips revealing teeth suggest an impatient lover who enjoys passionately rough sex. There may be a touch of hostility towards the opposite sex.

Missing teeth show a sense of urgency for an exciting varied sex life, motivated by fears of getting old, undesirable and impotent – a 'make the best of it while it lasts' attitude.

Fangs or sharp, pointed teeth indicate anger and belligerence expressed via a cynical or sarcastic sense of humour.

A large open mouth shows someone who loves the sound of their own voice – they will give you their opinion whether you like it or not. This compulsive talker is a poor listener who monopolizes conversation. Full of nervous energy, they like being centre stage and expect plenty of attention from their partner.

A small mouth is drawn by a discreet person who is not the sort to gossip or reveal confidences.

Lips with a thin and mean look reveal a critical nature and lack of sensuality. This person feels a mixture of guilt and resentment and is unable to express freely or receive heartfelt emotion. Consequently their lovemaking is lacking in spontaneity and warmth. This doodle generally signifies relationship conflicts and underlying hostility towards a lover or the opposite sex.

An extra-wide grin indicates someone who hides thoughts and feelings behind a mask of showmanship.

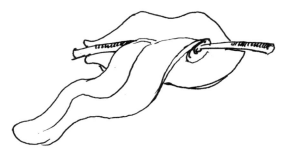

The tongue poking out of the mouth expresses hostility, impulsiveness and oral fixation. This individual, being highly sensual and a very skilful talker, thinks constantly about lovemaking and oral sex. When it comes to wildly arousing, erotic sex talk, you can be certain you are dealing with a virtuoso.

Ear

When doodled on its own, this is a message from the subconscious telling the person to listen to their inner self. If ears on a face are disproportionately large, this reveals hypersensitivity to criticism. One ear missing shows a cynical sense of humour. Both ears missing indicate a poor listener who may be absent-minded.

Jaw/chin

A jaw or chin that is very square suggests aggressive, domineering tendencies. Sharply angled, it reveals criticism of family and friends. A long and narrow chin indicates resigned, discouraged or sad feelings.

Freckles

These indicate a self-conscious nature and a desire to recapture one's youth.

Spectacles

Perhaps the subconscious is suggesting that a recent idea or decision needs closer examination? Spectacles doodled on faces in magazines or anywhere else also indicate a humorous, but immature, attitude to sex and relationships, reminiscent of a teenager. Although seemingly at ease, this person is actually emotionally and sexually withdrawn and unable to express openly sexual desires or heartfelt emotions.

Neck

An unusually long neck means the person is ruled by the head rather than the heart. An extremely short neck shows impulsiveness and stubbornness.

Hair

Human hair has great symbolic meaning. It represents freedom, individualism and strength, and sometimes (when shaved off or covered up) suppression of sexuality and devotion to a spiritual existence. In occultism it is regarded as one of the most extraordinary parts of the body. It belongs to the element Earth as it is solid and tangible; to the element Water because it is free and flowing; to the element Fire because it is fed from the furnace of the brain; and to the element Air because as it is light and can be blown by the wind. Hair is both living (because it grows) and dead (because it contains no nerves). It has its own life for it continues to grow after the death of the body – it is not surprising that hair doodles can be highly significant.

HAIR THAT IS FLOWING AND FREE

Free-flowing hair suggests a desire for emotional and sexual freedom, and a wish to express openly a warm, sensuous, loving sexual nature that is currently suppressed. With the right partner, this person will be refreshingly spontaneous and open-minded in lovemaking, free of the inhibitions and tensions inherent in most people.

HAIR THAT IS VERY SHORT, SPARSE OR BALDING

This indicates sexual inadequacy, frustration, and dissatisfaction with physical appearance.

MESSY-LOOKING HAIR

Suggests an unconventional, rebellious individual who is under a lot of pressure and feeling stressed.

SPIKY HAIR

This doodler is original, and likes attention. An alert, focused person who seems at the moment to be receiving insufficient warmth and affection.

CURLY HAIR

Indicates a romantic individual who wants to please others. They may be overloaded with too many ideas and too many worries.

ORNATE HAIRSTYLES

A sign of vanity, self-consciousness, aesthetic sensitivity and fashion awareness.

MOUSTACHE

Almost exclusively doodled by males. Indicates insecurity about sexual prowess and a desire to project a strong masculine image. Drawn on a woman's face, it shows a wish to change or devalue a specific female or perhaps females in general.

Beard

Shows poor self-esteem and strongly repressed emotions and thoughts.

Human figures

These can reflect how a person feels towards their own body as well as their current emotions and social attitudes.

People in a group

Drawn by a sociable person who feels a close sense of connectedness with other people.

Matchstick people

Frequently doodled by highly motivated individuals – often business executives – who want to make their mark on the world. This mature, independent-minded person is intelligent, opinionated, decisive and very direct. Their emotions are controlled, and they are interested in facts, not speculation. They possess initiative, recognize essentials and skilfully locate short cuts. They tend to neglect the needs and feelings of those around them.

GEOMETRIC PERSON

Figures constructed of squares, circles and triangles etc. reveal emotional over-control, a feel for form and structure and a very logical, responsible manner. This person values personal ambition far more than intimate relationships.

NAKED PERSON

Nude drawings symbolize strong sexual desire and openness and are often doodled by unconventional, inwardly rebellious individuals who want to be free of the constraints of sexual inhibitions and social pretences. This person desperately wishes their intimate relationships to be more sexually liberated and exciting. This doodle may also be expressing frustrated sexual desire for someone who is not currently available.

GIANT PERSON

Drawing someone who dwarfs in size the other figures in the same doodle often reveals a fear of the father. This person has a rebellious nature and an intense dislike of authority.

CHILDISH-LOOKING DRAWING OF PEOPLE

These reflect an emotionally needy, childlike nature.

TRAMP/VAGRANT

Reveals inner rebelliousness – a dislike of authority, rules and regulations hidden behind a façade of conformity. This person fears this **shadow** side of their psyche and often represses it. The 'Shadow' is a term used by Carl Jung to describe the darker more primitive aspects of human nature.

FIGURE CASTING A SHADOW

Represents the unknown, feared parts of the personality. This person is repressing the darker, instinctive aspects of their being. To evolve, they must learn to accept and assimilate this part of their psyche.

Person with a large torso and short skinny legs

This active, assertive, sociable individual is a smooth talker and appears to be confident. In reality, they are insecure, anxious and prone to overindulgence.

Person with large, solid hips and legs and a small torso

This person is not very assertive or expressive. They hold in their feelings and would rather listen than talk.

Large square-looking shoulders

These express hostility and an exaggerated desire for power.

Very rounded or fat person

Reveals a pleasant sense of humour and a friendly manner.

Muscular figure

A sign of physical and emotional self-absorption. This individual has developed a forceful, competitive, domineering personality in an attempt to compensate for underlying inferiority complexes and emotional insecurity. They may have an interest in weight training or bodybuilding.

ARMS SPREAD OUT WIDE

This person is friendly and eager to make contact.

ARMS RAISED IN THE AIR

This reveals anger and pent-up feelings of intense frustration.

LEGS

Long legs shows self-reliance. Short legs show insecurity. Tightly closed legs reveal inflexible attitudes and sexual inhibition.

PENISES

PENISES BY FEMALE DOODLERS

REALISTIC, FRIENDLY, OR FUNNY APPEARANCE

Discloses a keen sense of humour, sex appeal and a flirtatious manner. This person thoroughly enjoys socializing with men, and her attitude to sex is open-minded and light-hearted. Possessing a sensual nature, and a healthy sexual appetite, she is sure to be a good lover.

UNPLEASANT OR UGLY APPEARANCE

Signifies ambiguous feelings towards her lover or to men and sex in general. Sometimes she enjoys lovemaking and then, for no apparent reason, she becomes resentful towards her lover and disinterested in sex.

Penises by male doodlers

The following interpretations are only applicable if the doodle is habitual.

If a male regularly doodles a penis this usually discloses a penis fixation and latent bisexual or homosexual tendencies.

Realistic appearance

This person feels comfortable with his homosexuality.

Humourous appearance

This person may be repressing homosexual inclinations.

Ugly appearance

Signifies complete denial of, or a lack of self-acceptance for, homosexual inclinations.

Snakes

This classic archetypal symbol of the phallus and sexual prowess has been attributed, in many cultures, with occult, magical or psychic powers, great wisdom and considerable energy. This doodle always reveals a preoccupation with sex and the male sexual anatomy. It is sometimes doodled when the animal-like impulses of human nature are rejected by the conscious mind. The person who doodles snakes should remember that we evolve as humans, only when we learn to accept and assimilate the darker, more primitive side of our being.

SNAKE COILED AND READY TO STRIKE

Shows a defensive state of mind, ready to retaliate. The male doodler may feel his virility is being questioned, the female doodler may be feeling threatened by a sexually over-assertive man, or anxious and uncomfortable with male sexual arousal.

SNAKE ENTWINED AROUND PART OF A HUMAN BODY

Indicates a fear of being a slave to sexual passions. This person could be sexually overindulgent – a nymphomaniac or a male sexaholic – or ashamed of their carnal desires and sexually repressed.

SNAKE STRETCHED OUT TO FULL LENGTH

This person's sexual nature is flexible, open-minded and free from inner tensions.

SNAKE'S TAIL IS IN ITS MOUTH

Discloses a deeply passionate, highly erotic and sensual individual who is crazy about sex. Men and women who draw this doodle especially enjoy oral sex. These types are often aware of the mystical and spiritual connotations of the sexual union, and may well have a deep interest in Oriental sexual practices such as those described in the *Kama Sutra* or Taoist sexual yoga. Men who make this doodle have confidence in their own virility and know how to please a partner.

houses

A house is a complex symbol that can give clues about the doodler's attitude to home and family. The front of the house often represents the front or façade the doodler presents to the world and can reflect the intellect and psyche of the individual.

houses in general

People who habitually doodle houses are prepared to work hard to build a solid foundation to their career, social life and intimate relationships. They feel best being around family in the safety of their own home.

The sun shining above house and/or smiling figure in front of house

This signifies a harmonious family environment. It is a sign of contentment with family life.

Narrow, cramped-looking house

Discloses emotional repression, rigid opinions, tension, frustration and a lack of social ease.

House drawn proportionally with precision and good attention to detail

Reveals a good sense of form and structure. This person would suit a creative career in design or construction.

Large, showy house

Reflects strong ambition and a desire for high status, admiration and respect. This extroverted person enjoys being the centre of attention.

House surrounded by a wall, fence or garden

This person considers their home a secure refuge from the outside world. If the garden is an important feature of the doodle, it indicates a strong desire for financial security and material possessions.

House shaded black

This doodler has strong apprehensions about the future, economic problems or conflict in a relationship. Their poor self-esteem and pessimism is reducing their happiness and ability to cope with difficulties.

Damaged, cracked or crumbling house

Suggests emotional trauma. Reveals severe anxiety and an identity crisis.

Signs of repair

This suggests a subconscious wish to repair psychological damage.

Heavily shaded rooftop

A sign of difficulties in a relationship.

Chimney smoke that goes downwards

Indicates depression.

A wide-open door on a vacant house

Indicates a hospitable person who is feeling lonely and isolated.

House with no door

Signifies that this person is a real loner.

House with lots of windows

This person wants to know what is going on in the lives of everyone around them. They could be socially intrusive.

People looking out of the windows

Suggests a very friendly, sociable, family-oriented individual who is involved in numerous outside activities. Love and companionship is high on this person's priorities.

Castles

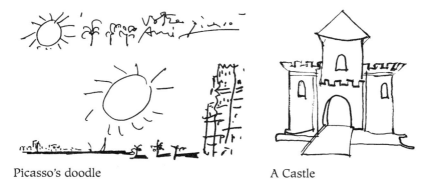

Picasso's doodle   A Castle

Show a respect for traditional values and history. This realistic, practical-minded person works hard to construct a secure material foundation. They are likely to have creative interests requiring good manual skills. At the moment they feel like escaping from the numerous dangers and insecurities of existence. Castle doodles frequently show optimism and a wish for status, wealth and elegant living.

NUMBERS

Habitually doodling numbers reveals an organized mind, mathematical skills and a preoccupation with financial matters. If, however, specific numbers are repeatedly doodled, see the following symbolic interpretations.

1 Egocentricity or loneliness or perhaps a desire for oneness, unity.

2 May represent conflict due to a Jekyll/Hyde split or difficulty in a making a choice? Perhaps this person feels inferior to a brother or sister.

3 Signifies a desire to overcome difficulties that are impeding progress.

4 Represents the four elements, seasons, dimensions, and points of the compass – in other words, where we are in time and space. Reveals a down-to-earth individual concerned with planning and organization.

5 Discloses a wish to forget past tensions by focusing on future goals. May disclose financial worries or excessive interest in money.

6 Suggests material desire, a collecting instinct, and possible jealousy.

7 Concerned about the passage of time and brevity of life. Goal-oriented.

8 Represents an awareness of infinity and a desire for personal evolution.

9 Signals the desire to unify the mind, body and spirit (the number 9 combines the feminine symbol of a circle with the masculine symbol of a vertical line).

10 Shows idealistic aspirations. In numerological terms, the number 10 represents the cosmos, law and order, and completion. The Hindus consider this the perfect number.

666 Believed by many to be the sign of the devil. May disclose anxieties or obsessions connected with black magic or other negative areas of occultism.

888 Believed to be the sign of Jesus. Reveals a fear of evil forces and a strong interest in spirituality and the art of psychic self-defence.

Arrows

Arrow doodles often reveal focused ambition and a very opinionated, analytical mind that is skilled in locating short cuts and solving problems.

Numerous heads

These are a sign of enormous persistence – this person never gives up once their sights are set on a goal.

Connected to a square

Denotes an intelligent, imaginative individual with many practical ideas.

Connected to a circle

Reveals a willingness to help others in trouble.

Enclosed inside something (e.g. cylinder/square)

Indicates a cautious nature and a perfectionist streak. This progressive, original thinker offers reliable advice and enjoys problem solving.

With two heads pointing in opposite directions

Shows indecision.

Pointing at an object

Suggests frustration or anger directed at this object.

CLUSTERS POINTING IN THE SAME DIRECTION

A sign of strong ambition, but efforts are not focused as there is no clear plan of action. This doodle frequently reveals a wish to punish someone.

SHADED-IN

Insecurity regarding an important decision.

POINTING IN MANY DIFFERENT DIRECTIONS

An exceptionally motivated, open-minded individual who is overloaded with ideas. This person often has trouble deciding which direction to take and tends to waste energy by trying to juggle too many projects simultaneously.

AN ARROW SUIT

This individual feels very frustrated and has a desperate need to escape from their current situation. They are not having much success in achieving their aims at the moment.

PRACTICE

When you next come across a doodle of a face, gaze at it gently, letting your awareness penetrate without judging or analysing. Stop after a while and write down your impressions. This will enhance your ability to interpret doodles on a purely sensory level – it will open the door to your intuition and **sixth sense**.

5 a helping hand to interpret doodles

*Y*ou do not need to read this chapter to use the rest of the book. The guidelines here can add more depth to the interpretations provided in the following chapters and will enable you to interpret any extremely unusual or unique doodles not featured in this book.

The role of intuition and logic in doodle interpretation

Although doodle interpretations should be based on the tried and tested information laid out in this book, the role of intuition should not be neglected. This invaluable sixth sense can help link into a comprehensive portrait the symbolic interpretations given throughout the book with the aspects of character derived from the principles in this chapter. In addition, intuition can sometimes inexplicably sense through someone's doodle into areas of the personality not apparently reflected in any physical aspects of the doodle itself.

Finally, you can use logical reasoning – Sherlock Holmes style – to piece together information in order to make further deductions. For instance, if a doodle reveals anger and a moody, changeable nature, then you can logically conclude (though this might not be reflected in the doodle) that this person does not sulk. Instead, they have angry outbursts that are over with quickly.

What is the difference between someone's regular doodles, and those they rarely produce?

If someone rarely produces a particular doodle, it will reflect only minor personality tendencies, or passing states of mind and short-lived emotional reactions. Doodles can change from one day to the next, influenced by unexpected occurrences or brief moods and fleeting thoughts. Conversely, doodles that are a regular part of a person's doodle repertoire usually reveal dominant and influential aspects of their personality, behaviour and attitudes.

How to spot romantic doodles

More frequently drawn by females, these doodles are generally produced by someone in love or in a romantic state of mind. Formed with soft, rounded harmonious looking strokes and light to medium pen pressure, they are quite easy to spot. They reflect things intuitively associated with romance, for example flowers or hearts. Alternatively, they may depict aspects of nature, or objects associated with childhood, that evoke pleasant feelings, such as bees, sunshine, or cuddly toys. Sensitive, receptive people who are able to co-operate with others often produce doodles like this: ruled more by their heart than their head, they are able to express freely their love and affection.

Detecting sexual doodles

Sexual doodles are not always easy to intuitively detect, although some – beds, breasts or lips for instance – are fairly obvious. Less recognizable are the symbols of virility in our society, such as cars, or objects that are prominent features of disco or party settings – cigarette lighters, lipstick, flowing hair, long eyelashes, etc. Certain doodles are classed as sexual because they are phallic symbols – numerous elongated objects such as rockets, spears, towers, pencils or animal horns fall into this category.

CONFLICTING MEANINGS IN DOODLES

If someone produces a number of different doodles that reveal a variety of seemingly incompatible characteristics, or if you find conflicting meanings within features on the drawing of faces, do not panic. Personality is often a complex mixture of contrasting traits. In such cases, often one doodle or feature stands out from the rest and will exert the main influence over the person's behaviour. Also remember that a person's habitual doodles will have a far stronger influence than those they rarely produce. If, however, none of the contrasting doodles fits this description, this simply indicates a natural shifting from one pattern of behaviour to another, depending on mood and situation. If these contrasting characteristics are extreme, you may even find a Jekyll/Hyde split. For instance, if a doodle reveals a romantic nature that desires a serious, long-term relationship, but another, belonging to the same individual, indicates a powerful desire for one-night stands, this person's desires and behaviour can alter dramatically. The latter desire may express itself merely in the person's fantasy, depending on circumstances.

INTERPRETING INK COLOUR

The descriptions in this section are applicable only if the doodler regularly chooses a certain ink colour out of strong personal preference. Royal or dark blue is not included because most people use this simply because it is standard.

Red

This reveals energy, ambition and sometimes an aloof, arrogant or condescending manner that hides low self-esteem. It can also indicate warmth and vitality, a desire for constant stimulation and a powerful sex drive. Watch out for a bad temper. This colour intensifies any emotions revealed in a doodle.

Pink

Females who opt for pink have good fashion sense and enjoy displaying their femininity. Harmony and understanding is especially important to them. Luckily their flexibility and receptivity minimizes any friction in their casual and personal relationships. Males who choose pink are very sympathetic and sensitive, but also vain, self-obsessed and easily hurt by criticism. Their **anima** (female side) is developed, so expect feminine mannerisms.

Black

Very career-minded people with conventional views and a sober, serious attitude tend to use black ink. Their awareness of life's hardships makes them prone to tension, anxiety and feelings of pessimism.

Light blue or turquoise

This person tries hard to avoid causing tension or conflict at work and in relationships. They have a strong desire and need for a peaceful lifestyle. There is a healthy balance between the feminine and masculine elements of the personality, a developed sense of culture, artistic inclinations and a reflective, introspective and spiritual approach to existence.

Grey

A goal-oriented individual with strong creative interests in fields such as music or writing. Inclined to cynicism and depression.

Brown

This is a rare colour, sometimes the choice of artists and graphic designers who have enjoyed successful careers. The doodler may have a keen interest in alternative lifestyles and ecology.

Green

Reveals an intense desire to be seen as unique. This individual tends to show eccentric behaviour patterns, has low self-esteem and is emotionally unpredictable. They are inclined to jealousy and resentment.

Purple

A rare choice of colour. This attention seeker has an air of self-importance and superiority that conceals feelings of inadequacy. They are interested in following a spiritual path. Expect moodiness, hypersensitivity to criticism and a rebellious nature.

The significance of positioning

The following applies only if the doodles were drawn on an empty sheet of paper.

Top of the page

Indicates imagination, optimism and enthusiasm. This person is inclined to daydream has an absent-minded streak, and is not very practical. They enjoy lengthy discussions.

Bottom of the page

This doodler tends to have pessimistic views. They are materialistic, and are interested mainly in productivity and accomplishment.

Centre of the page

Discloses a careful, security-minded, organized individual who is conscientious and clear thinking. This person likes plenty of attention and has a poised social presence.

Left-hand side of the page

This person is preoccupied with unhappiness experienced in their childhood or teenage years. Frightened of the future, they cling to the security of routine and the familiar aspects of their existence. A façade of self-assurance often masks their shy, socially reserved, private nature. They find it hard to establish new friendships and need plenty of reassurance from family and friends to help them express their potential.

Right-hand side of the page

This energetic, enthusiastic individual escapes unpleasant memories by focusing wholeheartedly on ambitious plans for the future. Impatient for success, they are often impulsive and will take risks to achieve their goals. Gifted with good communication skills, this friendly, open person feels at ease in social settings and enjoys the companionship of others.

EDGING — DOODLES SPREAD ROUND THE EDGE OF THE PAGE ONLY

Reveals a strong fear of venturing away from known and familiar things and people. This person tends to stay close to home, in the company of parents and a trusted social circle of old friends. They need encouragement to help them explore their potential.

WHOLE PAGE FILLED WITH DOODLES

This person lacks social reserve. Their manner of communication is intrusive and this can cause strong negative or positive reactions in others. They are very talkative and intensely dislike being alone. They tend to get involved in too many activities and become mentally overloaded with conflicting thoughts and emotions.

VERY LARGE DISTANCES BETWEEN INDIVIDUAL DOODLES ON A PAGE

A person who needs plenty of privacy and likes to keep a distance from others socially. This individual fears contact and closeness due to mistrustfulness.

BOXED-IN OR FRAMED DOODLES

Reveals strong caution. These types are very much on their guard around strangers, and are very concerned with constantly increasing their security.

VARIOUS DRAWING STYLES THAT CAN ADD TO THE SYMBOLIC INTERPRETATION OF DOODLES

HEAVY PEN PRESSURE

The meaning of any doodle is amplified if the person presses with their pen so hard into the paper that you can easily feel the indentations of the lines on the reverse side of the paper when you slide it between your thumb and index finger. For example, if the doodle reveals sexual dissatisfaction or hostility, then you can be certain that, with heavy pen pressure, the underlying sexual discontentment or anger will be intense. People who use a pen in this way are also forceful, determined, productive, highly energetic and prone to constant frustration.

LIGHT PEN PRESSURE

If the pressure is obviously light – so that it cannot be felt at all – this will considerably reduce the intensity of feelings expressed by the doodle. Erratic pressure – shifting between very light and very heavy – discloses an emotionally unstable, restless nature filled with fear.

SHADING

Doodles with a darkened appearance produced by heavy shading suggest feelings of anxiety, tension and unexpressed anger. Shading accentuates negative interpretations and reduces positive ones. For example, if a doodle symbolizes happiness, the anxiety revealed by heavy shading will considerably reduce or even neutralize the feeling. If pessimism is revealed then you can safely interpret depression.

Doodles drawn with a pen of choice that produces broad, thick lines or a smeary, smudgy appearance

Such a style intensifies any feelings revealed in a doodle – if a doodle's symbolic meaning discloses an aggressive nature and is also smeary, smudgy or drawn with a thick-nibbed pen, then expect uncontrollable anger that could be expressed physically. Alternatively, if the doodle reveals unhappiness, then look out for episodes of severe depression. Sexual interpretations of a doodle such as lust, passion, frustration or repression will also be intensified.

This doodling style always reveals someone with powerful sensuality and a strong, instinct-driven, earthy, passionate nature. This pleasure seeker is overindulgent. Their sexual feelings are very easily aroused and they often lose control over their intense emotions.

Doodles drawn with many sharp, jagged or spiky formations

Doodles that express negative emotions will have these feelings amplified by the presence of sharp, angular or spiky formations in the drawing. If seen in doodles that symbolize positive states of mind, then you should assume that the doodler has mixed feelings, both positive and negative – depending on mood. In addition, these graphic signs reveal an authoritarian, aggressive outlook on life, as well as stubbornness, inflexibility and a cuttingly sarcastic streak. This person resents authority and can be opinionated and argumentative. Strong-willed and competitive, they know what they want and do their best to get it. They can't relax, as they need constant activity to feed their active, analytical mind. In relationships they are domineering, intolerant and uncompromising.

Doodles formed with gently curved, soft lines and no noticeable sharp edges

Negative connotations of a doodle will be reduced, and positive qualities enhanced, if it is drawn with curved lines, rounded shapes and no jagged forms or sharp edges.

Large-sized doodles that take up a lot of space

These indicate strong ambition and a big ego that hungers for abundant admiration and respect. This enthusiastic person loves being the centre of attention and thrives on social occasions with their self-assured, theatrical, extroverted manner. Assertive, they have an original imagination, progressive ideas and a dislike of authority. They need a job with status, responsibility, variety and plenty of freedom – preferably in the public eye. In relationships, they can be affectionate and fun to be around, but if they feel insulted or things don't go as planned – watch out! This character can be egocentric, temperamental and very childlike – blowing up trivial occurrences out of all proportion.

Very small doodles

A sign of introspection, self-discipline and modesty. This person has sharp concentration, good organizational skills and a reliable memory. They can work alone in occupations requiring precision and close attention to small details (scientists often have tiny doodles). In relationships they can be rather pedantic but will avoid emotional confrontation. They enjoy communicating only with close friends.

Neat, precisely drawn doodles with great attention to detail

This alert, observant person has excellent concentration and memory, an uncanny eye for detail and plenty of physical and intellectual stamina. They are conscientious, punctual and highly organized – a genuine perfectionist. In relationships they may be irritatingly fastidious and fussy.

The same doodle repeated a great many times

This may simply reveal a temporary obsession with some worrying thought or problem. However, if this person always doodles this way it suggests an obsessive-compulsive nature. These types periodically become locked in irrational, compulsive behaviour patterns, or gripped by obsessional thoughts. They attempt to cope with anxiety and fears of failure by procrastinating, using routines and rituals that often have almost superstitious significance to them. If the repeated doodle is very jagged in appearance – watch out! This indicates fierce anger that is being suppressed, and the person may be looking for some excuse to let it out. They will inevitably explode with rage if they don't start dealing with these feelings soon.

Retracing many times over each doodle

Any form of retracing is a sign of anxiety, tension and guilt. It often occurs when someone is under great pressure or overworked. Those who don't like to delegate responsibilities frequently retrace. This characteristic should be taken as a warning to slow down.

ᴘʀᴀᴄᴛɪᴄe

1 When can one expect a possible Jekyll/Hyde split?
2 Use your intuition to make a short list of doodles that are likely to have romantic connotations. Do the same for sexual doodles. Look up the interpretations in the relevant chapters to check your results.

6 ABSTRACT/ GEOMETRIC DOODLES

*D*oodles do not need to resemble closely the examples provided for the interpretation to apply.

The significance of abstract and geometric doodles

The subconscious mind plays a key role in the production of doodles. This influence is at its strongest in abstract and geometric shapes – which is why they can be exceptionally revealing. In addition, these doodles are by far the most popular. Although the subject matter of doodling can vary enormously from person to person, almost everyone includes geometric or abstract shapes in their repertoire.

Lines

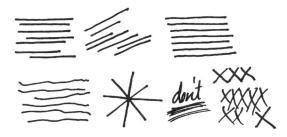

HORIZONTAL PARALLEL LINES

This person has good concentration and keeps a cool head in emergencies. They know what they want from life and have the motivation and determination to get it.

DIAGONAL PARALLEL LINES

A strong desire for leadership – in relationships they will want to be boss.

EVENLY SPACED LINES (HORIZONTAL OR DIAGONAL)

A highly conscientious person who requires their work to meet the highest possible standards – expect fussy, pedantic behaviour in their intimate relationships.

WAVERING HORIZONTAL LINES

These reveal mood swings and inconsistent behaviour patterns. This person is tense and anxious about the future and does not know which direction to take.

DISSECTING LINES

This motivated, focused perfectionist has a sharp mind and a persistent, determined nature that will ensure success.

UNDERLINING

Shows a desire to emphasize something that is terribly important to the doodler, and a source of tension for them. Excessively repeated underlining shows a pedantic, obsessive-compulsive worrier.

X-ING

In mathematics, X represents the unknown quantity. It also has religious connotations associated with martyrdom. This person has strong beliefs – philosophical or religious – and experiences guilt, which makes them self-destructive at times. Their outlook on life is pessimistic, possibly due to death anxiety caused by the loss of someone close. They simultaneously fear extinction, and are attracted to its mystery.

Loops

Loops demonstrate an attempt to unwind from current stresses. This calming doodle reveals a desire to switch thinking off and feeling on.

Large wide loops

Reveal a highly active imagination and a need to express bottled-up feelings. Capable of being sympathetic and compassionate, this person is very sensitive to criticism and can become highly emotional when under pressure.

Distorted looking loops

Suggest emotional disturbance and difficulties relating to other people.

Very narrow loops

Disclose an emotionally suppressed, secretive nature filled with fear, insecurity and low self-assurance. This person has difficulty relaxing and feels self-conscious and tense in social settings.

Flowing figure 8

Reveals the desire to develop a harmonious, balanced, relaxed attitude to existence. This friendly, peaceful person has a vivid imagination, good aesthetic sense and a persistent nature.

REPETITIVE PATTERNS

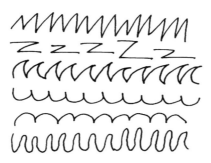

ZIG-ZAG/JAGGED FORMATION

Reveals hostile and possibly vengeful feelings at the time of the doodle. This person has an ambitious, aggressive fighting spirit and a desire to lead. Assertive and opinionated, they can't stand orders and are easily provoked to anger. Hard-working and with a precise, logical, analytical way of thinking, they will be domineering and critical of those who do not conform to their way of thinking. This person needs to cultivate more tolerance.

Z SHAPES

Full of energy, this alert, persistent fighter is ready to tackle any obstacle on the road to achieving their ambitions. When they are angry, expect them to show a fierce temper, cuttingly critical language and a vengeful attitude.

SHARK'S TEETH FORMATION

Reveals a strong fighting spirit and an ability to tell a convincing white lie to get out of a difficult situation. When angry, this person can be very critical and fault finding.

FLOWING CUP SHAPES

This doodle shows a flexible, friendly, sympathetic social manner and a strong need to be accepted and liked by others. This person is talkative, generous and has a good sense of humour. Possessing a natural sense of rhythm, they are likely to enjoy physical activity.

FLOWING ARCHES

Show a strong sense of pride and creative imagination, reliable intuition and a tough, loyal nature. Such doodlers are very private and wary of strangers – they hide their emotions and are secretive about the past. Their controlled, conventional social manner, conceals an eccentric outlook on life.

FLOWING PHALLUS SHAPES

Reveal a vivid erotic fantasy and unconventional sexual tastes.

THREE-DIMENSIONAL FORMS

Three-dimensional doodles indicate a sharp analytical mind, a creative imagination and a good potential capacity for three-dimensional visualization. This person is organized, plans well, and is skilled at dealing with problems – they are able to view situations from all possible angles. They may well have a strong appreciation of architecture and design.

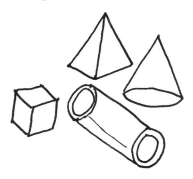

Boxes/Cubes

Doodles of boxes and cubes indicate a practical-minded, realistic person who strongly values security and will work hard to create a solid foundation in their career and relationships. They possess a focused, methodical mind, are resourceful and imaginative and are able to plan and organize with efficiency and vision whilst dealing with any problems. They always weigh up situations carefully before taking action. They will be interested only in serious long-term relationships with loyal, emotionally mature partners.

Pyramid

Symbolizes mystical powers. This person wants to explore fully their creative potential and capacity for self-awareness and spiritual growth.

A female pyramid doodler reveals an appreciation of the mystical nature of sex, and a fascination with the mysterious nature of femininity. A male pyramid doodler discloses a changeable sexual nature – ranging from warm, compassionate and loving, to hostile and intolerant, when sexual needs are not fulfilled.

Cone shapes

Indicate sexual tensions that are not finding adequate release. This creative person is struggling to decide which direction to take.

Tubes

A practical-minded, clear-thinking individual with a peaceful nature. This person is not suited to high-pressure working environments.

Geometric forms

If any of the following are drawn three-dimensionally, see also *Three-dimensional forms*.

TRIANGLES

UPWARD-POINTING

Symbolizing the masculine and the element Fire, this suggests a probing mind, searching for answers. Intellectually thirsty, perceptive and analytical, this person enjoys a challenge. They prepared to take risks and has very strong will power and a forceful nature that can't be pushed around. Decisive and independent, they will not compromise once their mind is made up. Expect them to be bossy and critical towards partners who fail to satisfy their needs.

LINKED TOGETHER SIDE BY SIDE

Softens the aggressive intensity of characteristics associated with triangle doodles – reveals a more relaxed, balanced nature.

TRIANGLE INSIDE A CIRCLE

In addition to the triangle characteristics reveals an avid truth seeker interested in personal evolution.

EXTENDED AND POINTING TO THE LEFT

Reveals bitterness and resentment towards people and events from the past. This is wasting precious intellectual and emotional energy.

DOWNWARD-POINTING

Symbolizing the feminine and the element Water, this suggests someone far more passive and less ambitious than those who doodle upward-pointing triangles. The intellect here is focused unsuccessfully on a search for emotional and personal meaning, rather than material success. Very self-critical, this person's approach to love is lacking in sensuality and feeling, as they are trapped in their heads and emotionally detached. They may suffer great disappointment owing to their over-idealistic search for the perfect mate.

TRIANGLES INSIDE TRIANGLES

Reveals insecurity and defensiveness, as well as sexual frustration and bottled-up anger that is periodically released via outbursts of cutting sarcasm.

SQUARE

Symbolic of firmness and stability. This person is straightforward and unpretentious, interested in concrete facts and practical goals. Possessing plenty of common sense and a strong motivation to build a secure life, you can be sure they will have a responsible attitude to their career and other duties. They have a serious attitude to love and believe strongly in building long-lasting relationships and close family ties. The square indicates firmness, practicality, stability and logic; a person who is earthy, practical, methodical and stubborn.

SQUARES WITHIN SQUARES

Reveals strong caution, insecurity and a wariness of strangers. This person feels frustrated, trapped and overloaded with problems – literally 'boxed in'.

CIRCLE

A universal symbol representing eternity, wholeness, unity, perfection and protection. Of all the mathematical shapes, the circle is the most symmetrical – it has no ends or corners. The cycle of life in the universe has often been represented as a completed circle – the movement from non-ego in the womb, through ego, and back to non-ego. In mysticism, the soul is also attributed with having a 'round form' (Jung). Circles reveal a strong desire for psychological wholeness. They signal the need to listen to one's inner wisdom, creativity or potential for growth. The person who draws circles has a strong potential to harmonize the male and female elements of their psyche, which will improve emotional balance and creative output. If the circles are very accurate they are making good progress. If wobbly, or not very round, this suggests many lessons still need to be learned.

The habitual circle doodler is essentially a sincere, kind-hearted, loyal individual with a sense of humour and a playful, loving streak. They feel comfortable expressing and receiving love and affection and are looking for the sort of deep connection and love that can only be found with partners interested in long-lasting companionship.

If any of the following circle doodles are applicable, then add their corresponding meanings to the above.

NARROW OR POORLY FORMED CIRCLES

Indicate stress and anxiety due to work or relationship.

CIRCLES IN NEAT ROW

Suggest an orderly mind – someone who does what they need to do in a gentle, unhurried manner.

CIRCLES WITH DESIGNS, SHAPES AND FACES INSIDE

A highly creative, imaginative person with a very private nature – someone who dislikes intensely being questioned about their private life.

CIRCLES WITHIN CIRCLES

Reveal someone who feels under tension that is making them emotionally vulnerable. To cope with the situation they have become very cautious and are temporarily withdrawing into their own private world.

OPEN CIRCLES

This talkative individual tends to monopolize conversations and likes being the centre of attention. They are openly affectionate in relationships and expect their partner to be equally demonstrative.

OTHER GEOMETRIC SHAPES

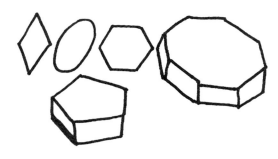

DIAMOND

Reveals an analytical, inquisitive, ambitious character with a forceful personality. This person suffers from insomnia due to a restless mind.

EGG

A potent and ancient symbol. In Hindu, Chinese and Greek mythology it was believed that all creation emerged from a Cosmic Egg. Egg-shaped doodles may signal the start of an important creative enterprise, or perhaps an inventive solution to a baffling problem.

HEXAGON

If precisely drawn with all sides of even length, this reveals a highly organized, ambitious person with clearly set goals.

OCTAGON

If precisely drawn, this indicates very good concentration, close attention to detail and a first-class sense of form and structure. This intelligent, scientific thinker is a perfectionist who can solve complex problems.

PENTAGON

This diplomatic, tactful individual is a good negotiator who knows just how to handle people in order to achieve a desired objective.

STARS

These symbolize high aspirations and hopes. Stars always reveal an idealist with strong ambition, aggression and the persistence to fight for what they want from life. This person has a tough side that won't allow them to be pushed around.

FIVE-POINTED STAR (PENTAGRAM)

Symbolizes the four elements – Fire, Water, Earth, Air – and also the spirit. A sign linked to witchcraft it frequently reveals an interest in New Age thinking and occultism. This doodle reflects a subconscious (and maybe also a conscious) desire to achieve balance and harmony between the forces of thinking, feeling, sexuality and the survival instinct.

SIX-POINTED STAR (HEXAGRAM)

Also called the Star or Seal of Solomon, this symbolizes balance between the masculine and feminine elements of human nature. The upward triangle signifies the masculine, the downward one the feminine. Six-pointed stars disclose good concentration and a highly inquisitive and exploratory style of thinking.

STAR ON THE TOP OF A CHRISTMAS TREE

Extra motivated – this character knows precisely what they want out life and exactly how they intend getting it.

CROSS

For thousands of years the cross has been considered a highly potent symbol of wisdom, mysticism and spirituality amongst the Egyptian, Chinese, Hindu, European and many other civilizations. As a doodle, it often reflects a message of hope and inspiration from the subconscious during a difficult time. It may also represent the realization that going through a period of self-denial or self-sacrifice is necessary for the achievement of certain goals. If doodled in multiples, it shows emotional insecurity and a desire for protection from negative forces.

ANKH

This shape is associated with Atlantis and ancient Egypt. It symbolizes existence – the loop symbolizing the feminine, the T-shape the masculine; it also symbolizes initiation, as its shape suggests a key. This doodle discloses New Age or occult interests as well as enthusiasm and optimism for the future.

LIGHTNING

Reveals someone prone to flashes of insight, inspiration or awareness. This person gets extremely enthusiastic over new ideas or realizations that pop into their head. This doodle may reflect guilt feelings as well as anger and fear. This dominant person is alert, intelligent and very impatient. They want things done 'quick as a flash' and feel irritable when kept waiting.

SPIRAL/COIL/SPRING

Suggests an insecure, worried and anxious person who often broods over problems. This person is secretive, emotionally guarded and sexually repressed. In relationships they hide from lovers, troubling thoughts and feelings to do with sex. They fear rivalry and easily become jealous, though they may hide this. This person needs someone who can offer them protection and security. Spirals that begin from the centre and move outwards suggest very strong psychic tension and a need to unwind. Spirals that move from the periphery inwards reveal a need to gather together scattered physical, emotional and intellectual energy into a single point of focus directed towards a specific goal or activity. You'll need to ask the doodler which was the starting point for the spiral – the centre or the periphery.

SWIRL

This looks like a storm formation on a satellite weather photo. It shows a great deal of dynamic energy that currently has no direction.

ABSTRACT DOODLES

ABSTRACT DESIGNS

Intricate patterns made up of numerous different, connected abstract designs are a sign of stress that is causing mental overload. This highly intelligent person has abundant creative potential that has not yet found an adequate outlet.

ERRATIC SCRIBBLES, SQUIGGLES OR ABSTRACT DOODLES WITH NO PATTERN

A definite sign of tension, anxiety, moodiness and poor concentration, stemming from an inability to deal with a difficult problem or decision. This independent, imaginative, free-spirited individual dislikes routine and structure. At the moment, however, they need this sort of organization to deal with the mental overload of thoughts and feelings that is causing their confusion and inability to deal with reality. If heavy pressure is used, or the doodle has a darkly shaded appearance, then the individual is carefully hiding their disturbed mental state from those around them.

CROSSHATCHING

Signifies anxiety, tension and sexual frustration. This person can't relax, as they are preoccupied with inescapable problems and responsibilities, connected with daily survival. When this doodle is drawn over something, it suggests a wish to forget or escape the influence of whatever it is covering.

Maze

Symbolizes the complexities of existence. This person feels trapped, frustrated and overburdened with problems and responsibilities that seem unavoidable.

Mosaic

A sign of obsessional thinking. Perhaps this person is looking for some creative inspiration to complete a current job.

Shapes constructed with dots

This reveals a patient, hard-working individual with excellent mental focus and good powers of observation. They notice the smallest of details and will have a fantastic memory for facts relating to work and personal interests. If the shapes are precisely and proportionally formed, then this person will be able to use their hands creatively to perform fine precision work.

Games

May represent an attempt to make light of the conflicts and hardships of existence by treating life as a game.

Noughts and crosses

Reveals a competitive nature. Win lines indicate a sense of optimism; stalemate suggests someone who is resigned to living with unfulfilled ambitions and desires.

Chessboard/Checkerboard

A very masculine doodle. The black and white squares may represent an awareness of the battle between good and evil in life, or the subconscious conflict between opposing forces in the personality – creative and destructive, male and female, etc.

Intelligent, practical, emotionally controlled and a skilful communicator, this person enjoys challenges and is talented at solving problems. They possess sharp concentration, an eye for detail and an ability to organize and plan with efficiency and vision. Driven by a desire for substantial success and material security, their moods fluctuate regularly between periods of elation and discouragement depending upon how well they are progressing towards their goals.

Snakes and Ladders

This person wants to reach the top at all costs, even if it means behaving in a ruthless manner. They have a pushy ego.

A Number Board

This reveals an objective individual with a streak of cynicism towards anything that cannot be backed up by facts. They are financially very motivated and are likely to possess good mathematical and calculating skills. In their business dealings and personal life they are open and direct.

PRACTICE

Do any of your abstract doodles reveal tension or anxiety? Are you perhaps juggling too many things simultaneously? Is there anything you can give up with no negative repercussions? If so, take action!

ANIMAL/INSECT DOODLES

Doodles do not need to resemble closely the examples provided for the interpretation to apply.

The significance of animal doodles

These doodles reveal a love of nature and animals. They also frequently express subconscious feelings towards parents. Male animals sometimes represent the father; female or very small animals often symbolize the mother. Wild or ferocious animals can reveal repressed instinctive urges and sexual impulses that are potentially destructive if ignored.

Interpretation of animal doodles

Bear

This person still feels a strong bond with their mother.

BIRDS

Birds in flight: Shows a vivid imagination, a need for freedom, and high-flying ideals or spiritual aspirations – a wish to transcend earthly problems. Also reflects a love of travel and adventure and a light sense of humour.

Flock of birds: The desire to feel part of a group or to have many friends.

Birdhouse: A determined, forceful, practical individual who can't be pushed around. A high pedestal reveals high ideals.

Bird's nest: Symbolizes the desire to start a family and provide for the future. A strong caring instinct.

Cock: In ancient mythology, the cock represented vigilance against danger. In a doodle it denotes a subconscious warning to beware of someone or something in one's current dealings. It may also reflect confidence and happy news.

Dove: Symbolizes the spirit, and is associated with peace, hope and love (see *Swan*).

Eagle: Discloses pride, confidence, perceptiveness and ambition to reach the heights and to control others. This person is a tough survivor.

Owl: A symbol of wisdom and awareness. This person is cautious, modest, observant and very private. Their imagination constantly generates original ideas so they need periods of contemplation and meditation.

Penguin: At a subconscious level this doodler realizes that their problems are not as serious as they seem – if they keep cool, things will work out fine. This person's sense of humour helps them through times of trouble.

Swan: Symbolizes serenity, purity, peace and monogamy. This compassionate faithful human being loves nature and respects all living creatures. Intelligent and imaginative, they have a demanding conscience and a clear sense of right and wrong. Their relationships are fulfilling.

Bull

This animal represents the need to release repressed anger that could become self-destructive. A female doodler has mixed feelings of admiration and resentment towards macho men. A male doodler has a virile, confident manner that hides feelings of sexual inadequacy. Long horns denote a complex about genital size. An aggressive expression reflects frustration and resentment towards a lover.

Camel

Indicates someone who feels overwhelmed by problems and responsibilities.

Cat

A peace-loving romantic who loves animals, is loyal to friends in need and is easily hurt by criticism. A male doodler has feminine sensitivity. A female doodler seeks luxury and comfort and takes pride in her feminine sexual allure. If the cat's face is not visible, this denotes a lack of self-assurance. A curly or wagging tail shows a great sense of humour.

Cow

An ancient symbol of motherhood, this reflects kind-hearted, nurturing behaviour, and warm feelings towards the mother.

Crab

This person is cautious, defensive and ready to retaliate.

DOGS

Usually doodled by females, this doodle reveals loneliness and a desire for true companionship. This person is a loyal friend and a romantic, faithful lover. Bared teeth signify anger over betrayal or a childhood fear of dogs.

Doghouse: This is a sign of relationship conflicts that need to be dealt with.

DOLPHIN

See *Porpoise*

DRAGON

A universal symbol of good (in Eastern oriental cultures) and evil (in Western cultures). If you are from the Far East, your dragon doodle suggests a desire for supernatural powers and esoteric knowledge. In Western cultures, this doodle discloses the risk of damaging physical and psychological health if repressed anger and fear is not dealt with soon. This person is frightened of the destructive consequences of surrendering to powerful sexual impulses and is terrified of death, though they may block this from conscious awareness. A dragon with wings signals the ability to overcome this conflict through spiritual development.

ELEPHANT

Symbolizes the radiant self. To someone familiar with the Hindu religion, this represents inner strength that clears all obstacles. Ganesha, the Hindu elephant god, is the great obstacle – destroyer. This crafty, humorous person may bend rules and tell white lies to achieve objectives. This doodle may also reflect a fear of being overweight.

Fish

A religious fertility symbol suggesting optimism and personal growth. This person rises to challenges and has reliable intuition.

Frog

Reflects a strong desire for personal transformation and an improved lifestyle. This person feels unattractive and suppresses erotic desires through fear of rejection. They tend to joke about their own shortcomings, attempting to hide their inferiority complexes behind humour.

Giraffe

Reflects an immature sexual nature. This person feels comfortable only with partners who joke around when they make love. Ruled by their intellect, they have difficulty expressing deep emotion and passion.

Goat

Symbolic of sexual and creative energy, virility and lust. Hard-working, intelligent, inquisitive and stubborn, this person believes in the supernatural and is aware of the dark side of their nature. They often feel and express intense lusts. If, however, the goat is tethered to a post, then they are not expressing this sexuality – either because of sexual inhibitions or because of an unsatisfactory relationship.

Hedgehog

Reflects a warm, loving nature protected by caution and mistrust. This person hides their deeper emotions behind a cynical sense of humour, and if annoyed or criticized they respond with cutting sarcasm and backhanded compliments.

Hippopotamus

A message from the subconscious to slow down and relax.

Horns

Although tuned into their sexual feelings this person still feels sexually inadequate because of current difficulties they are facing – the horns of a dilemma.

Horse

Symbolic of masculine power and sexual prowess and the desire for more freedom. This person has strength of character and high ambition – a perfect recipe for success. They enjoy helping others with psychological support or advice. A female doodler wants men to accept her as an equal. She has a healthy sexual appetite but is frustrated because she demands too much from her lovers. She expects them to be incredibly passionate, understanding, super sexy, and totally faithful – an almost impossible combination. A male doodler dreams of increased virility and sex appeal. He is energetic and passionate but restrains some of his sexual desire for fear of losing complete control. His **anima** (female side) is developed so he will be kind and sensitive.

Winged horse: Reveals a poetic imagination.

Darkly shaded or black horse: Represents depression and fear of losing control over passions and instincts.

Lamb

Symbolizes vulnerability and dependence – the child within that needs love. It may also reflect their innocence – the beauty of the doodler as they were before the innocent joy of being, gave way to the confusing complications of doing, getting and achieving.

Lion

Symbolizes devouring appetites and lust for power. This strong-willed, independent thinker has imagination, resourcefulness, plenty of energy and high aspirations. They are sociable and will strive to achieve a position of authority and distinction that commands admiration and respect. They fear being taken over by their high sex drive, or by aggressive and self-destructive impulses that occasionally pop up from their unconscious mind. In males, there are mixed emotions of love and fear towards the father. In females, there is an active animus (male side), which often reflects a wish to be king of the jungle/office/house.

Lizard

Symbolizes the repressed aspects of this person's shadow self that they want to ignore. Also reflects an awareness of the cold, unfeeling side of human nature.

Monkey

A lively individual with a good sense of humour and fun. Sometimes childish, even infantile, they definitely prefer 'monkeying around' to facing up to life's responsibilities.

Mouse

Signifies a vulnerable, modest person who would like to develop a more confident, less fearful approach to life.

Octopus

Represents a possessive mother
or mother-attachment that is
preventing this person
from developing
their own
individuality.
They lack a clear
sense of direction
because they try to juggle too many goals.

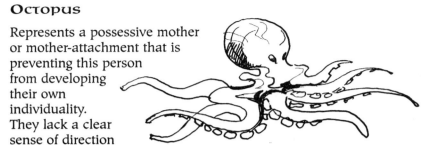

Pig

Symbolizes recognition of unattractive qualities, and a desire to get
rid of them. This person is self-conscious about their figure and
inclined to dieting, which is difficult as their willpower is erratic
because of a lazy streak. Luckily a good sense of humour helps
them to cope well with failure.

Porpoise

Sensitive, idealistic and with a powerful love of nature, this
ecologically aware individual adores animals and is honest and
loving in relationships. They are attracted to meditation and New
Age interests.

Rabbit

This may signify a desire for children. Also reveals an inquisitive
nature with good intuition and spiritual insight.

Rat

Rats for many people symbolize dirt and disease. This doodle may
disclose a person's guilt about some real or imagined misdeed as
well as a fear of illness and death. Alternatively it could represent
rejection of parts of this person's psyche that they find unattractive.

Shark

This is a subconscious warning of dishonesty from friends or associates – the person needs to be extra cautious in financial dealings. Signifies a constant fear of financial troubles. Also shows a strong awareness of the dark side of the psyche.

Sheep

A sign that this individual is being over-influenced by convention and other people's attitudes. They need to establish a more independent way of living.

Snail

Represents feminine sensitivity and emotional insecurity. This person is careful and cautious in words and action and sexually inhibited. Secretive and emotionally repressed, they find sex talk very embarrassing and have a fear of rivalry that makes them easily jealous, though they may hide this fact.

Squirrel

Often a symbol of acquisitiveness. This person is insecure of the future and is wondering how to create a secure foundation to their existence.

Tail

Prominent tails on any animal denote a keen sense of humour that is likely to have a strongly sexual tone.

Tiger

This individual has great respect for and fear of their instincts and sexual desire, which they often restrain.

TORTOISE/TURTLE

A symbol of longevity, consistency and endurance. Denotes a careful, methodical, persistent character who is modest and reliable.

UNICORN

A symbol of purity and spirituality that reveals a streak of idealism and optimism and a youthful, innocent attitude to existence. This person feels that beneficial changes are occurring – that something mystical or magical is taking place in their life. Perhaps an end to the tension between the female and male energies in the psyche, or the acceptance and assimilation by the conscious mind of the darker forces of animal instinct.

WHALE

This individual feels they have a protective influence surrounding them. Alternatively, this doodle symbolizes a dominant mother whose influence is preventing this person from developing as an independent being.

ZEBRA

A creative, original personality who stands out from crowd.

The significance of insect doodles

(The following does not apply to bees, butterflies, caterpillars and ladybirds.) An insect doodle often discloses an unhealthy attitude towards sex and a fear of being ruled by this primal force. It indicates a person who suffers guilt (consciously or subconsciously) whenever lustful, erotic thoughts or feelings grip them. Consequently they are unable to enjoy the pleasure of sexual arousal. Instead, during lovemaking they tend to 'separate' or detach from the experience, observing it from outside with an attitude of disapproval.

Interpretation of insect doodles

Ant

A messenger from this person's subconscious, telling them to listen to the 'still small voice' of their inner self. This well-organized individual escapes their fears via total immersion in hard work. They often feel insufficiently rewarded for their endeavours.

Bees

Signifies a healthy attitude to relationships and sexuality. Love, sex and romance, rather than money or career, is undoubtedly at the top of this person's list of priorities. They know how to enjoy fully all the sensual pleasures of food and sex, and in lovemaking they are sensitive and considerate.

BEETLE (ALL BEETLES EXCLUDING LADYBIRDS)

This person feels ashamed of their sexual feelings, which they consider embarrassing and dirty.

BUTTERFLY

This person wants to trade their routine way of living for a more meaningful and peaceful existence. Although warm and sensitive, they do not like to commit themselves and will therefore tend to change relationships and hobbies quite frequently.

CATERPILLAR

This modest person is carefully and steadily working on their own personal growth and transformation.

LADYBIRD

Reveals feminine sensitivity coupled with a pleasant sense of humour. This softhearted romantic is careful not to hurt or offend others.

SCORPION

This individual fears being betrayed by someone close to them, whom they resent, and are ready to strike back at in self-defence.

SPIDER

Sometimes symbolizes influence by a domineering mother – a wish to break the power that she still has over the psyche if it is stunting personal growth, inhibiting the ability to express individuality or affecting relationships with the opposite sex negatively. It may also indicate the feeling that one is in a dangerous, apparently inescapable situation. Heavily shaded or black spiders indicate overwhelming feelings of pessimism.

SPIDER'S WEB

This person has a devious nature and a calculating mind, but at the moment they are anxious and highly frustrated because they feel trapped and threatened by their current existence, and can't seem to find a way out. This feeling might stem from a restricting job or family life, or from conflicts in an intimate relationship.

WASP

See *Scorpion*.

ThE a-z OF DOODLES IN GENERAL

*L*ook up the hidden meaning behind a person's doodles in this alphabetically arranged, easy-to-use dictionary. It covers all relevant aspects of personality and behaviour, including sexuality, romance, aggression and intelligence. Doodles that you cannot find in this dictionary can be found in the following chapters: Chapter 4 (Complex doodles), Chapter 6 (Abstract/geometric doodles) and Chapter 7 (Animal/insect doodles). Doodles do not need to resemble closely the examples provided for the interpretation to apply.

Abstract patterns: See Chapter 6.

Aeroplane: (see also *Phallic symbols*) Usually doodled by males. This person daydreams about escaping all their responsibilities to find complete freedom in some faraway place. A war plane reveals anger and frustration.

Aerials (television): Indicate ambitious ideas and an important decision.

Aliens/abduction (beamed into spacecraft): Does this reflect an apparently real experience? If not, then this person needs to change their attitude dramatically – they are overwhelmed by fears connected with work and/or intimate relationships.

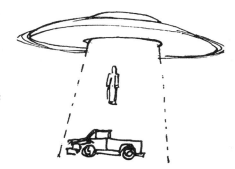

Almond: A female doodler is self-conscious about her naked body. A male doodler views the female body as a mystery.

Alphabet: Doodling many letters reveals a tidy, organized individual. Just one or two letters shows a preoccupation with numerous responsibilities.

Anchor: A sign of unresolved parental conflict and a desire for someone or something to believe in – a wish for more peace and stability.

Angel: Usually doodled by females. Indicates a romantic, enlightened attitude and a longing for increased spiritual awareness – perhaps for guidance from a guardian angel? This person sees lovemaking as a mystical union that connects one with the universal self. If the drawing is heavily shaded or black, the above does not apply, as this denotes depression arising from broken hopes and dreams. In males this doodle may indicate bisexual feelings.

Animals: See Chapter 7.

Ankh: See Chapter 6.

Apple: A magical fruit and potent symbol. In Greek myth it symbolized love and desire; in Christianity, temptation and loss of innocence. Apple doodlers are thoughtful, loving and idealistic with a mature attitude to sex and deep respect for nature. See also *Food*.

Arrows: See Chapter 4.

Baby: Discloses a gentle, romantic nature and a love of children. May also represent some new talent or idea that needs nurturing and developing.

Ball and chain: This person is feeling depressed due to seemingly insoluble problems.

Baggage: Symbolizes old habits and attitudes that need to be dropped and a desire to alter one's life. Sometimes it is a sign of depression, following recent loss or separation.

Ballerina: A feminine, idealistic individual who still keeps their childhood dreams alive. This person has a cultured, romantic view of life, love and relationships.

Balloon: Reveals a loving, childlike personality with refreshing innocence, enthusiasm and humour.

Bambi: See *Disney characters*.

Basket: A progressive thinker who is friendly, generous and receptive to new ideas.

Bathtub: An expression of guilt. A desire to slow down and relax. Discloses a need to get rid of habitual negative attitudes/habits/emotional reactions.

Bed: Possibly a complaint from the subconscious about bad-quality sleep. This person loves comforts and sensual pleasures. Lovemaking is their oasis – an escape from life's pressures.

Beer mugs: Usually a male doodle. This person loves social drinking and flirting with the opposite sex. They may misinterpret a friendly smile as an invitation for romance.

Bells: A time-conscious, punctual individual who is preoccupied with sex.

Bicycle: A productive, hard-working individual who adores nature.

Boat/yacht: Reveals a desire for adventure – an escape from the pressures of work and family to find peace of mind. Large liners also suggest a love of luxury.

Bomb: A sign of hostility – a desire to cause damage to someone. Also symbolizes fears of death, or feelings of helplessness in the face of explosive emotional conflict.

Book: Reveals a desire for knowledge, wisdom and understanding and an aptitude for learning, research and problem solving.

Bottle: Signifies inhibitions – 'bottled-up' emotions.

Boots/shoes: Usually doodled by females. A sign of sexual frustration and desire for a super-sexy lover. Heavy boots show a wish to dominate lovers. Sharp pointed heels or toes demonstrate sarcasm and bitchiness. A shoe that is detailed with shoelaces shows feminine sensitivity and a pedantic nature.

Bow-tie: A tidy, artistic individual who wants admiration. A female doodler needs a very secure relationship to enjoy sexual intimacy. A male doodler needs reassurance to overcome fears of inadequacy.

Bowl: See *Cup*.

Bracelet: See Chapter 6 (*Circles*).

Brain: Indicates an intelligent, inquisitive, scientific-minded intellectual. Emotionally controlled and detached.

Bread: An age-old symbol of life. This person sees their role as provider or 'bread winner'. They are in hot pursuit of financial stability.

Breasts: A female doodler is self-conscious about her bust size or desires motherhood. A male doodler is emotionally dependent, immature and attracted to women with a maternal nature. Especially aroused by all the oral aspects of foreplay, he has a preference for women with large breasts.

Brick wall: A practical-minded, methodical individual with a materialistic, down-to-earth streak and a love of possessions.

Bridge: Suggests the presence of an obstacle that must be overcome to facilitate an important period of transition.

Broom: Reveals regret – a desire to sweep away past mistakes.

Bubbles: Indicates an enthusiastic, friendly individual. Connected bubbles reveal a good organizer; disconnected bubbles reveal a **disorganized daydreamer.**

Cactus: In a female doodler, a cactus denotes sexual frustration, and aggression or mistrust towards a lover or men in general. Uncomfortable with male arousal, she often avoids lovemaking, which she considers more pain than pleasure. The male doodler feels that sex is  dirty and is ashamed of his sexual impulses, which he restrains rather than enjoys.

Cage: This person feels restricted, confined and angry in their career or personal life.

Cake: Discloses satisfaction with work and social life. This friendly, hospitable character treasures intimate and casual relationships.

Candle: The female doodler is fascinated by the male anatomy. A small candle indicates a lack of interest in size – a large candle reveals preference for well-endowed lovers. Dripping wax suggests suppressed lust, which she fears to unleash. A male doodler suppressed his arousal  during childhood due to sexual guilt. Consequently he is now obsessed with sex, penis-fixated and prone to regular erotic dreams. If the candle drips wax then he favours autoeroticism and may have bisexual tendencies.

Cannon: See *Gun*.

Car: Almost exclusively a male doodle. Discloses an impulse to get away and a love of travel. A prominent exhaust indicates an obsession with sex, and genital self-confidence. These types need the buzz and excitement of a

varied sex life, as they are addicted to the thrill of impressing new lovers.

Cards: Depending on which suit is doodled, this indicates problems in one of the following areas: *Hearts*: love and relationships; *Diamonds*: financial matters; *Clubs*: responsibilities and new enterprises; *Spades*: health and enemies.

Cartoon characters: See also *Humpty Dumpty*. Indicates a vivid fantasy and lively sense of humour. This person enjoys relating jokes and amusing true events, and is fun to have at parties. A friendly person who focuses on the bright side of life.

Cash: If this person doesn't stop worrying about money and security they will damage their physical and psychological health.

Cell bars: See *Cage*.

Cemetery: A sign of pessimism and depression – possibly caused by a recent bereavement. This person is preoccupied with death and may be repressing a traumatic memory from early childhood. They need to beware of their self-destructive impulses. If gravestones are heavily shaded the doodler is feeling resentful towards someone.

Chain: The doodler feels imprisoned by problems or responsibilities. They may be facing obstacles that are blocking their progress.

Chair: Suggests a desire for more comfort, rest and leisure time.

Chessboard/Checkerboard: See Chapter 6 (*Games*).

Cheese: This person is overloaded with numerous everyday worries.

Children: See *Baby*.

Church: This person is struggling to resolve emotional conflicts and find peace of mind.

Cigarette: For a cigarette smoker this is an emergency health warning from the subconscious to give up this habit. For non-smokers, it represents frustrated sexual feelings. Smoke rising from the tip reveals optimism that things will improve; sinking smoke signifies the reverse.

Cigarette lighter: This person has a one-track mind, caring only about dating and sex, attracted to singles bars and exciting, erotic one-night stands rather than serious relationships. Males who draw heavily shaded cigarette lighters may forcefully coerce unwilling partners into sexual submission.

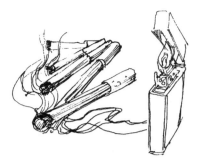

Cliff: Symbolizes a turning point in life. The cliff edge may be the 'end of the road' – a subconscious signal that it is time for some radical changes.

Clocks: May be a subconscious message to stop wasting time. This person is acutely aware of how quickly time passes and how short life is, and they wish there were more hours in the day to get things done. Simultaneously they resent 'living by the clock'.

Clouds: Clear, fluffy clouds reveal a sympathetic, kind-hearted daydreamer who is content with their current existence. Clouds that are shaded or black reveal tension and mood swings and a fear of danger on the horizon. This person is depressed because of relationship problems that seem inescapable.

Clover: A sign of optimism for the future.

Clowns: This person enjoys telling funny stories and being the centre of attention, but low self-esteem and sad feelings are concealed behind this cheerful front. If the clown's face is frowning then they are also feeling especially disappointed with their current circumstances.

Coffin: See *Cemetery*.

Compass: This person feels they are headed in the wrong direction and wants to make some major changes in their life.

Cotton reel: Reveals a love of the arts and a desire to explore potentials and talents to the full.

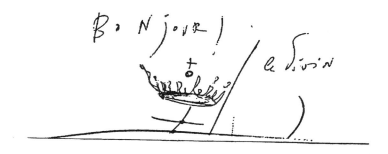

Dali's doodle

Crown: Reveals a huge ego. This very confident individual desires endless wealth, power and authority. They can be very critical and domineering.

Crown of thorns: An individual who is obsessed with death, has poor self-esteem and is judgemental and intolerant of others.

Cuddly toys: See *Teddy bears and cuddly toys*.

Cup: This person is helpful and hospitable, sincere and uncomplicated. In relationships they are warm, sensual and sexually open-minded.

Cupid: Signifies an overwhelming desire to find happiness in relationships. This romantic idealist is sensitive, and inclined to be in love with love.

Curtain: Denotes a desire for more privacy and personal space.

Daisy chain: See *Flowers*.

Dartboard: Demonstrates a goal-oriented, competitive nature that thrives on challenges. This person has a sharp mind and a persistent nature.

Desk: See *Table*.

Devils and gargoyles: Signify repressed guilt. This person restrains their sexual impulses, as they fear being controlled by carnal lusts.

Dice: This down-to-earth individual plays to win and takes risks, but only after carefully calculating the odds.

Disney characters: Discloses an immature, childlike streak and an intense dislike of responsibilities and duties. In relationships, this individual is loving and loyal with a great sense of humour, but also emotionally demanding.

Doll: See *Baby*.

Donald duck: See *Disney characters*.

Drum: This repressed person has difficulty expressing their angry feelings.

Dynamite: See *Bomb*.

Earrings: This self-conscious person is observant and has a good sense of humour.

Envelopes: *Blank envelope:* signifies someone who is waiting expectantly for an important letter. *Address on far right:* shows someone trying to forget some trauma from the past. An impatient, impulsive nature. *Address on far left:* this person is frightened of the future and of change. A person trapped by habits and routine. *Address in centre:* a well organized, poised, friendly social manner. *Address at bottom:* pessimistic attitude to existence. Undergoing a period of depression.

Eye: See Chapter 4.

Face: See Chapter 4.

Fan: An appearance-conscious, poised individual with a respect for tradition.

Fashion doodles: This artistic, creative-minded person is over-concerned with appearances – with the 'container' rather than the 'contents'. They need to develop a more evolved view of themselves and the people with whom they associate. A male doodler may be revealing homosexual inclinations.

Feather: Indicates non-materialistic intellectual or creative aspirations and a cultured, intelligent, light-hearted attitude to life.

Feet: An honest, direct individual with earthy, passionate desires, and a straightforward, unromantic approach to sex. Omitting feet on otherwise complete figures reveals emotional instability or pessimism.

Fence: A fence doodler is a guarded, introspective individual who avoids confrontations. This person is sexually inhibited and frightened of losing control over primal instincts. Sharp-pointed tops on the fence reveal the capacity to be cuttingly sarcastic.

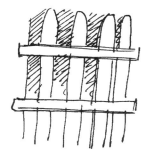

Fingers/thumb: See also *Phallic symbols*. An upward-pointing finger reveals a domineering, ambitious, proud nature.

Fire/fireplace: Discloses a hospitable home lover who enjoys the company of family and friends. This person can be very loving, romantic, sensual and passionate but when annoyed has a fiercely angry, unforgiving temper.

Firecracker: This doodler is extroverted, impulsive, pushy and hyperactive.

Fishing rod: An ambitious, persistent individual who likes the outdoor life.

Flags: Signify pride and a desire for attention and victory. *Triangular flag:* denotes a competitive, forceful nature, a sharp analytical mind and an impatient and irritable character. *Square flag:* signifies a practical-minded, careful person with a sensible, security-conscious attitude to life. *Chequered flag:* suggests an insecure, indecisive personality in whom creative and self-destructive impulses conflict with one another. *Heavily shaded or black flag:* indicates someone under great pressure, with problems at work and/or personal relationships. This person is feeling anxious, insecure and depressed.

Fleur-de-lis: This was the emblem of French kings and it discloses a sensual nature with a strong sense of culture and an interest in history.

Flowers: Often the doodle of someone in love who has a very childlike, innocent side to their nature. Their attitude to sex and relationships will be charmingly refreshing, though adolescent and immature at times. This sentimental, compassionate, romantic person is only able to really enjoy sex if it goes hand in hand with deep feelings of mutual love. In relationships they will be loyal and faithful – and devastated if a partner deceives them.

Food: Doodling fruits, vegetables and other types of food discloses a warm, hospitable nature that hungers for a more satisfying sex life. This person has a healthy sensual appetite and is inclined to erotic daydreaming, so their lovemaking is bound to be open-minded. Clearly they will harmonize best with sexually active lovers.

Fountain: Symbolic of 'the fountain of life', this reveals a kind-hearted soul who values existence and tries to be pleasant and useful to others. This doodle also reflects a fear of ageing and a desire to remain young and sexy.

Framing: Drawing an edge or frame around doodles reveals a wish for a more self-disciplined and organized existence.

Funnel: This person has numerous ideas that need sorting out.

Gallows: An indication of a person who needs psychotherapy to release intense anger and hatred.

Garbage: A sign of an overloaded mind. This person is tired of their belongings, friends and lifestyle and desperately wants to change direction.

Gate: This individual feels the need to protect themselves and those close to them. They want to leave the past behind and start a new life.

Ghosts: Represent fear of being controlled by the unknown and a mixture of apprehension and fascination towards occultism. This person has a shy, private side and is self-conscious – easily embarrassed by mistakes.

Golf club: Indicates a love of this sport and the outdoor life. See *Phallic symbols*.

Goofy: See *Disney characters*.

Grapes: This sensual pleasure-seeker is very friendly and hospitable, but possesses a strong jealous streak that will emerge in their intimate relationships. See *Food*.

Gravestones: See *Cemetery*.

Grass: Denotes a romantic nature-lover who is searching for tranquillity.

Guitar: Discloses a love of music and female beauty, and also a youthful flirtatious nature. See also *Musical instruments*.

Gun: A female doodler feels hostile towards her partner or men in general, and suffers from penis envy – she desires the advantages and power that men are perceived to possess. A male doodler feels sexually inadequate and suppresses his sensitive side to appear more 'macho'.

Hair: See Chapter 4.

Halo: Symbolizes the true self – the source of all wisdom and power.

Hammer: Signals a tough person determined to succeed. See *Phallic symbols*.

Hand: A single hand suggests a charitable, peaceful nature with strong faith. Very big hands disclose an impulsive, forceful personality. Very small hands signal low confidence, and social uneasiness. Absence of hands on a complete figure indicates sexual frustration.

Handcuffs: Reveals guilt and a desire for punishment over recent bad conduct.

Hang-glider: Reflects a longing for inner peace and freedom. A subconscious request to make time for relaxation and meditation.

Harlequin: A suggestion from this person's inner self to trust their intuition about a particular person or situation.

Hats: Often the sign of a sensitive person with friendly manners. A very large hat is a desire for status, authority and admiration

Heart: See Chapter 4.

Helicopter: Reflects strong indecision.

Horseshoe: This person needs some good luck and wants to be out of the rat race. *Pointing upwards*: reveals hope and optimism. *Pointing downwards*: signifies depression due to a spell of bad luck.

Hot-air balloon: An optimistic, enthusiastic, adventurous individual, full of original ideas and happiest when using their creative, artistic imagination.

Hourglass: Discloses a fear of ill health, ageing and death – the feeling that time is running out. This doodle shows impatience with progress towards goals and worries that money is running out; a desire to make footprints in the sands of time – to achieve something noteworthy. If the sand is all in the bottom half it indicates regret over mistakes and lost opportunities.

House: See Chapter 4.

Humpty-Dumpty: This individual is great fun to be with when things are going well, but easily upset and knocked off balance by even small reversals in luck.

Ice-cream cone: This fun-loving person is crazy about food and sex. A warm, sensual lover who adores all the oral components of foreplay.

Initials: If someone doodles their own initials, it shows egocentricity and a desire for status and public recognition. This person wants to make their mark on the world. Their charisma and confidence disguise fears of failure and feelings of inadequacy. They need plenty of approval to boost their self-esteem. Doodling someone else's initials reveals a desire to get closer to them. Doodling a partner's initials indicates lovesickness and emotional insecurity.

Insertion doodles: Any doodle incorporating pairs of objects in which one goes inside another. The objects may be drawn side by side or already connected to one another. Examples are: key and lock; train with tunnel; bolt and nut; arrows and quiver; bee feeding from flower; lipstick protruding from its holder. Such doodles are a sign of powerful sexual desire that is not being satisfied. This person may be 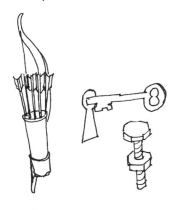 coping with their frustration by releasing it through hard work or via some physical or sporting activity.

Iris: This symbol of hope reveals a sensitive, sensual individual who spends much time thinking about sex. Their approach to lovemaking is likely to be warm, gentle, sensuous and romantic.

Island: This person feels lonely and isolated.

Ivy: The enduring nature of evergreens suggests this person's deep respect for the qualities of loyalty and fidelity and long-lasting relationships.

Jack-in-the-box: Signifies an impulsive, playful, childlike individual who loves surprises.

Jar: See *Cup*.

Jewellery: Reveals ambition, showiness, and materialism. This person will consider only jobs offering a high salary, and they believe that expensive gifts are the only reliable sign of genuine romantic love.

Jug: See *Cup*.

Key/keyhole: Symbolizes wisdom, freedom and a turning point in life – the desire to leave the past behind and make a new start. May represent the key to happiness or the solution to some problem or obstacle blocking progress. Is this person's subconscious offering them access to their true self or the key to someone's heart and sexual passions?

Kites: Symbolize a desire to escape responsibilities or some restrictive situation. Idealistic and ambitious, this person is reaching for the sky. If the kite string is close to the ground, then goals are practical and achievable. Strings far from the ground disclose a restless dreamer with unrealistic aspirations.

Knot: A sign of unfinished business that needs to be dealt with. Also reveals a persistent, determined nature.

Ladder: See *Stairs*.

Landscape doodles: A family-minded individual who feels a strong affinity with nature.

Leaves: Denote a genuine nature lover. *Leaves with sharp points (e.g. holly):* demonstrate a tough personality with a sarcastic streak and cynical sense of humour. This person finds it difficult to relax and is easily irritated; a fault-finder who intensely dislikes being criticized. *Leaves with rounded or curved edges:* signify a friendly, laid-back, helpful person with a

sense of humour and good imagination. This warm person thoroughly enjoys their comforts and leisure time. *Marijuana leaves*: signify someone who is still psychologically addicted to marijuana even if they don't currently smoke it.

Light bulb: Symbolic of understanding and intuition. Reveals a need for more love and social contact and a desire for personal growth.

Lighthouse: Symbolizes a yearning for inner tranquillity.

Lily or lotus: The doodler has a strong craving for purity, innocence and spiritual growth.

Lips: See Chapter 4.

Logos: Distorting a company logo on a letterhead is a sign of dissatisfaction and insecurity concerning current circumstances. Shading in a Logo indicates depression and indecision – this individual does not know which direction to take. Aesthetically embroidering a logo demonstrates someone who is satisfied and comfortable with the current situation.

Lucky charms (wishbone, four-leaf clover etc): This person is desperately hoping for a stroke of good luck to come their way. See also *Horseshoe*.

Machine parts: Reveals attention to detail, manual dexterity and emotional self-control and discipline. This person has the potential to achieve well in technical jobs.

Mandala (a round form with design inside): Reveals a deep interest in self-exploration and personal evolution – the desire to find the true self.

Mask: This person is extremely private and hides their true nature behind a convincing façade. The doodle is a warning from their subconscious to 'unmask' and show their real face, or they risk losing contact with their true self. Doodles of tragi-comedy masks are a sign of disturbance due to a Jekyll/Hyde-type split.

Matchbox: This practical-minded person has original ideas and enjoys working with their hands.

Medicines: Pills, medicines, creams, etc. are the doodles of someone overly anxious about their health: possible hypochondria.

Mermaid: This person is preoccupied with finding an ideal lover. A female doodler is expressing insecurity about her femininity and fears of sexual frigidity – perhaps due to conflicts in a relationship. A male doodler feels rejected and lonely.

Microphone: Indicates a wish for more attention, a fear of not being assertive enough and the desire to acquire power over others.

Money (notes, coins): Reveals a desire for enormous financial success to compensate for feelings of inadequacy. This person finds it hard to express openly positive emotions. Obsessed with personal ambition, they pay little attention to their partner's feelings and needs and will often seem emotionally detached or cold.

Money symbols (dollars, pounds etc): (This is not applicable to those who use these symbols as part of their job.) Denotes dissatisfaction with the current standard of living and a strong desire for great wealth. Linking money signs together discloses someone who just loves a bargain.

Monster: Represents a person's fear of the unknown forces of their shadow self. They need to learn to accept and assimilate this part of their being if they wish to grow. They currently feel unbalanced and overburdened with monstrous problems.

Moon: Symbolizes spiritual renewal. A message from the subconscious that personal growth can be achieved only by listening directly to intuitive understanding which is the source of all spiritual wisdom. This romantic, passionate individual sometimes tries to 'reach for the moon' – to grasp the unattainable. *Crescent (new moon)*: an ancient symbol of moon goddesses – hence the custom of wishing on a new moon. This person is ardently wishing for someone or something to happen in their life. *Crescent facing left*: shows a need to re-evaluate one's goals. *Crescent facing right*: show that goals are clearly sighted.

Mickey Mouse: See *Disney characters*.

Motorcycle: Symbol of masculine strength and sexuality. This adventurous person loves speed, admiration and feels dominant, powerful and daring.

Mountains: Discloses idealism and spiritual or material ambition. This person loves nature and challenging goals. *Shaded mountains*: indicate depression, overreacting to difficulties – 'making a mountain out of a molehill'. *Round-topped mountains*: works methodically towards ambitions. *Jagged-topped mountains*: indicate someone who is extremely determined, who will fight ruthlessly for success, whatever the price. *Standing at the peak of high mountains*: shows a search for a deeper meaning to existence, a desire to reach the top.

Mushrooms: Denote secretiveness and caution – a very private nature.

Musical instruments/musical notes: Reflects creative potential in the arts, as well as a lively sense of humour, good intuition, sensitivity and a keen interest in music. Symbols such as treble clefs and notes are commonly doodled by musicians and composers.

Naked figures: See Chapter 4.

Names: *Doodling your own name*: indicates self-absorbtion and egocentricity; a search for a deeper sense of personal identity; a desire for admiration, respect and recognition – to be the centre of attention. If the name is doodled very large it also shows natural showmanship. *Encircled name*: shows a person with low self-esteem, cautious, wary and mistrustful – on the defence against attack. *Doodling someone else's name*: denotes concern or curiosity about that person. *Letters filled in*: indicate secretiveness, insecurity and anxiety concerning future prospects.

Necktie: A female doodler reveals her desire to be accepted by men as an equal. She may have repressed bisexual inclinations. A male doodler feels insecure of his organ size and sexually inadequate.

Nest: See Chapter 7 (*Birds*).

Noose: Indicates depression and guilt, causing self-destructiveness and suicidal thoughts. Alternatively, this doodle may signify repressed anger and a subconscious wish to do someone else harm.

Oasis: Denotes feelings of isolation. This person is insecure of their partner or close friends.

Ornate objects: Objects of any type that are embellished reveal an exhibitionist who tries to be the centre of attention.

Padlock: *Lock without a key*: this person feels trapped in a situation or excluded from one. *Lock with a key*: this person is ready to let someone into their life.

Parachute: A safe escape from recent problems or a subconscious warning of danger on the horizon. A longing for adventure but fear of the unknown.

Peeping Tom: Discloses a secretive, emotionally controlled individual with a strong sexual appetite and fantasies. Unfortunately, even when a relationship is harmonious they feel sexually frustrated as they cannot help thinking about others who might have an even more satisfying sex life. The male doodler is very attracted to pornographic films, magazines and erotic literature, though he may be too embarrassed to admit to this.

Penis: See Chapter 4.

Phallic symbols: Usually a male doodle. Examples include the following: aeroplane, baseball bat, fishing rod, animal horns, lighthouse, lobster, motorbike, pencil, pillar, rocket, spear, steeple, tower. These symbols all reveal a sex drive that is not being satisfied. This person tries to relieve their sexual frustration via erotic fantasy. If the phallic symbol has a damaged or weak appearance, it indicates fears of impotency or an actual sexual problem that is impairing performance.

Pineapple: Suggests a hospitable person who anticipates a happy social life.

Plants: This person feels a deep connection with nature which they see as a key to inner growth. See also *Leaves*.

Prison: A person who feels controlled by others, or perhaps trapped by fear and guilt.

Queen: Symbolizes this person's mother, who still plays a very important role in their life.

Question marks: Reflect a difficult dilemma or indecision over an important choice. This rational, logical person has humour, initiative and a pushy, persuasive way of extracting information from others.

Rainbow: A universal symbol of hope and promise. This kind-hearted daydreamer has realized that life rarely meets with one's expectations but, trusting in the goodness of human nature, they remain hopeful and optimistic. Spiritually aware, they are loving and faithful in relationships.

Rain: A sign of depression. Rain from a dark cloud reveals recent misfortune or unhappy relationships.

Rays: Rays radiating in shaky or wavering lines suggest a lack of direction and low energy levels. Steady, vital-looking rays disclose assertiveness, initiative and loads of energy.

Religious imagery: Reveals aggressive impulses that have been transformed into self-sacrifice – this person goes out of their way to help those in need.

Ribbon: Shows aesthetic sense, mental focus with attention to detail, and a happy state of mind.

Riding doodles (horse, bicycle, motorcycle, etc.): See *Insertion doodles*.

Ring: A symbol of commitment – hope that an intimate relationship or long-lasting friendship will endure.

River: Symbolizes the life force and the twists and turns of fortune. This person relies on their sense of humour to deal with life's ups and downs.

Robot: A subconscious message that this person should let their actions be guided by conscious awareness and intuition rather than habit-driven routine.

Rocket: Reveals ambition and clear goals. Possibly a news junkie who loves adventure and futuristic magazines. See also *Phallic symbols*.

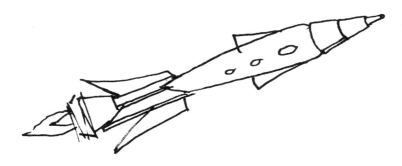

Roller coaster: Indicates sexual frustration and relationship difficulties. Sometimes this person is excited or euphoric – then, without warning, angry or depressed.

Rolling pin: Suggests a need to beware of impulsive actions inspired by temper.

Rose: A romantic, passionate perfectionist in search of an ideal existence. Rose with thorns demonstrates awareness and experience of great suffering.

Ruler: A conscientious, organized person with many responsibilities.

Saucepan: See *Cup*.

Saxophone: Discloses a love of music, especially jazz, and a sexy, sensual nature prone to overindulgence. See also *Musical instruments*.

Scales: Drawn with balance and precision, these indicate a sharp, precise intellect that carefully weighs up all the pros and cons before making choices. Scales off balance indicate anxiety and indecision regarding a worrying matter.

Screw: Denotes suppressed anger and resentment. This person is handy with repairing things.

Scroll: An intellectual individual with high aspirations and a strong interest in history and tradition.

Sea: Symbolizes life and the human psyche – the depths of the subconscious. It represents this person's creative and spiritual potential. Perhaps a message that they should be making more use of their abilities.

Seesaw: Indecision with regards to some person, idea or action.

Seashell: A love of beauty and truth. This person sometimes feels a need to completely withdraw from life to restore their energy.

Sharp weapons: If these are not normally a part of this person's doodle repertoire they probably indicate only short-lived anger, perhaps in the aftermath of a heated argument or recent break-up. Any violent feelings will, hopefully, remain unexpressed and fade away rapidly. If, however, someone habitually draws knives or axes, scalpels, cleavers, machetes, saws, scissors, swords, etc. – watch out! In this case the battle between the creative and destructive forces – between Jekyll and Hyde – has ended, and an exceptionally nasty Mr Hyde is now in full control. This emotionally disturbed person has a violent temper and is sexually frustrated. They have a callous, sadistic streak and feel very hostile towards their partner, and in some cases, the opposite sex in general. Their anger is rooted in repressed childhood hatred towards a parent figure. It causes them to shift between feelings of love and extreme hate, and they often wish great harm to others. If lacking in emotional control, they may violently abuse their partner – or in some rare cases, become self-destructive to the point of suicidal behaviour. Such doodles often appear in letters or drawings by criminals who have been convicted of exceptionally violent crime. If someone you have just met habitually draws sharp weapons do not take any chances – cease contact with them immediately.

Shield: Denotes a person with a sense of authority who feels the need to protect themselves from someone or something.

Ship: This is a signal from an individual's subconscious telling them to go ahead with recently made plans, whilst paying close attention to any potential problems involved. This person loves travel and tranquillity and urgently needs a holiday.

Shorts: This person has a childlike side to their personality, and nostalgia for childhood experiences.

Skeleton: Reflects the need to reduce some complex situation or argument to the bare essentials. Discloses a deep fear of death.

Skull: A symbol of mortality that is telling this person to reflect more on death in order to develop a more fruitful perspective on life. *Skull and crossbones*: this person feels tied down by their current situation. Luckily a strong awareness of death periodically gives them the courage to take chances and explore their numerous changing interests.

Smoke/smoking: Rising smoke reveals optimism that things will improve. Sinking smoke signifies the reverse. *Smoke from a chimney*: suggests anxiety connected with family life. *Smoke from a pipe*: suggests sexual anxiety.

Snake: See Chapter 4.

Snowman: See *Disney characters*.

Spectacles: See Chapter 4.

Spoon: Indicates optimism that security and happiness are just around the corner.

Sphinx: Reveals a fascination with the mysterious occult forces of existence.

Spiral: See Chapter 6.

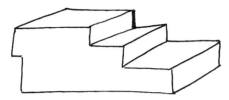

Stairs: Symbolizes progress. This self-assured, assertive individual has strong ambition and leadership qualities and loves challenges. They will work hard to achieve social status and wealth. Their views are rather rigid, and they often feel sexually dissatisfied.

Star: See Chapter 6.

Submarine: A subconscious suggestion that this person needs to examine closely their feelings to resolve an emotionally disturbing problem.

Suitcase: The time may now be ripe for some significant changes.

Sun: Symbolizes creative energy, life force and the light of consciousness. *Smiling sun*: indicates a kind-hearted dreamer with disappointed expectations but hope and optimism for the future. This person still trusts in the goodness of human nature and the potential for increased spiritual awareness. *Sunrise*: symbolizes the awakening consciousness, new realizations and new beginnings. The time is right for this person to explore their creative and spiritual potential. *Unhappy, frowning suns or sun that is almost obscured by clouds*: indicate depression – the individual is going through a stressful, unhappy period due to job-related problems or emotional and sexual frustration in relationship. May also relate to a need for emotional warmth from the father. *Darkened sun*: suggests profound depression.

Superhuman figures (hulk, superman, etc): This person escapes problems of existence and feelings of inadequacy through their fantasy, where they can play their ideal role of super-powerful, super-rich, super-lover.

Syringe: Denotes an intelligent, focused, analytical mind that is ambitious and calculating. This person has a cold, unemotional, clinical manner that lacks humour. They intimidate others with cutting sarcasm.

Table: Signifies a methodical, practical-minded, hard-working individual, with a potential talent for creating, constructing or repairing.

Target: This ambitious, focused, motivated person has their goals clearly in sight, and they won't give up until they hit their target.

Teardrop: Indicates feminine sensitivity, emotional vulnerability and a loyal, loving nature. Easily hurt, this person becomes extremely sad if mistreated. To find contentment they need an especially kind-hearted partner.

Teddy bears and cuddly toys: Indicates a soft, affectionate nature and an immature, adolescent attitude to sex and relationships. This person is attracted to lovers who act as a parent substitute. Emotionally dependent, they need plenty of cuddling and other demonstrative affection.

Telescope: Represents an intelligent, focused mind. This modest person sees their own life in relation to existence as a whole. They are interested in astronomy.

Tent/tepee: A tightly pegged-down, sealed tent indicates a guarded, cautious, private individual. An open tent suggests good-humoured hospitality.

Tornado: Signifies emotional conflict – especially anger and confusion.

Traffic lights: Active and productive with plenty of initiative, this person is direct in communication and good at locating short cuts.

Train: In youngsters, this denotes a wish for power and independence. In adults it means you are right on track with your ambitions.

Transvestite: A male doodler reveals his desire to display his feminine side, and possible homosexual inclinations. The female doodler reveals a cynical sense of humour and possibly resentment towards men in general.

Tree: See Chapter 3.

Tulip: The flower of eloquence and spirituality. This person is expressive, idealistic, romantic and a seeker of spiritual enlightenment.

Tunnel/black hole or dark passage: This individual is depressed and looking for an escape from troubles – a regressive desire to withdraw from the outside world, back into the security and comfort of the womb.

UFOs: This person's subconscious is informing them that in the depths of their true self there exists a superior intelligence and wisdom.

Umbrella: Indicates a fear of bad luck and a wish for protection and shelter. This secretive, cautious person can't relax and enjoy life as they are always on guard.

Vagabond: See Chapter 4 (*Tramp/vagrant*).

Vampire: Discloses anxiety, resentment and emotional conflict; also, temptations or ambitions that are immoral or unethical. This opportunist takes advantage of other people's vulnerabilities. In relationships they are angry, cuttingly sarcastic and sexually dissatisfied.

Vase: Denotes a good-hearted, friendly individual with a warm, sensual nature. *Nicely arranged flowers*: suggests creativity, imagination, orderliness, and sociability. *A single flower:* shows excellent taste, an extremely tidy, emotionally mature person with a clear sense of direction, intelligent and socially highly selective. *Messy flowers*: indicates a disorganized, easy-going hospitable nature.

Vegetables: See *Food*.

Violent scenes: Usually doodled by men, this danger signal should not be ignored. It would be wise to steer well clear of anyone who habitually produces these doodles. This person is sexually and emotionally extremely disturbed and frustrated – their mind is constantly filled with violent fantasies. Such doodles are often the choice of sadistic, violent criminals. See also *Sharp weapons*.

Violin: Indicates a passionate, highly sensitive individual with a love of music and probable musical talent. See also *Musical instruments*.

Volcano: Represents a potentially dangerous situation that is being ignored. A sign of suppressed frustration, anger or guilt that will erupt sooner or later in a very destructive fashion if it is not dealt with.

Water/waves: The source of all life, water is perhaps the most important of all symbols, signifying the mother, renewal, rebirth and destiny. On the deepest level, this doodle may represent a person's search for a deeper

meaning to existence – a desire for increased spiritual awareness. *Calm water*: reveals a light sense of humour and a kind-hearted, contemplative mood. *Messy and disorganized waves*: show indecision and a worried, confused, over-emotional state of mind. *Sunken objects*: often indicate anger or feelings of helplessness and depression.

Water tap with flowing water: Reveals an eccentric sense of humour, a sensual nature and a constructive creative mind.

Weapons: See *Sharp weapons*.

Wheels: The subconscious is requesting this person to look inside to find their true self. Also shows a strong feeling of being ruled by destiny. A steering wheel is a message to take control of one's life. At the moment this doodler feels frustrated, weighed down by responsibilities and ties that are slowing their progress and restricting them from expressing their creative potential.

Whips: Indicate sexual frustration, anger and a cruel streak in the personality. In an intimate relationship this may manifest as sadistic or masochistic behaviour and eroticism.

Wings (attached to an animal or human): Reveals a daydreamer with a vivid fantasy who wants to escape the responsibilities of everyday existence. This person is trying to develop detachment in order to gain better perspective on life problems. May also indicate a readiness to 'take off' on some important new project. Sometimes reveals spiritual aspirations or a desire to excel over others to compensate for underlying low self-esteem. On the physical plane, it denotes a powerful desire for the ecstasy of sensuality and a more liberated sex life.

Witch: If pleasant looking, this symbolizes inner wisdom and the capacity for self-healing and spiritual growth. If ugly or frightening it is a warning to watch out for the repressed, destructive elements of the ego – in a man, the negative aspects of his anima (female side), in a woman, the destructive forces of her animus (male side). Witches may also portray someone the doodler believes is untrustworthy or even wicked. A witch on a broomstick denotes the doodler's wish to travel or explore new dimensions – to fly to the highest peaks spiritually, materially or sexually.

Wizard: This person feels that occult forces are guiding their actions.

Word doodles: Large words doodled with double lines reveal a big ego that seeks attention, admiration and respect. This person has a creative imagination, progressive ideas and a rebellious nature that dislikes authority. In relationships they can be affectionate and good fun, but also egocentric, temperamental and childlike.

PRACTICE

1 Many doodles in this chapter reveal relationship conflicts. Is there some area of your relationship that is causing problems? Do your doodles shed any light on this situation? If so, then perhaps they can open the door to discussion between you and your partner.
2 When you analyse a doodle, use your logical/analytical mind – Sherlock Holmes style – to deduce *secondary* characteristics from the *primary* characteristics provided in the doodle interpretations in this book. For a more elaborate explanation of this method, see Chapter 5.

9 ThERAPEUTIC DOODLES

Certain doodles can significantly improve psychological well-being as well as physical co-ordination – hence the name 'therapeutic'. Even spontaneous doodles often have beneficial effects: when we are stressed they can relieve tension and act as an escape valve for restrained feelings of frustration, anger or impatience. The repetitive lines and shapes typical of many doodles help us to relax and to collect our thoughts together. This makes our thinking clearer and more effective.

WhAT ARE ThERApEUTIC DOODLES?

Therapeutic doodles are specially selected doodles that are used on a daily basis to enhance all the effects described above. The concept of this practice arose primarily from the work of two eminent French professors, Dr Pierre Janet and Professor Charles Henry, who were conducting research into human behaviour at the Sorbonne University in the late 1930s. They observed that, when various patterns and geometric shapes were repeatedly drawn for a specific time each day, this produced impressive physical and intellectual improvements in their test subjects.

In 1910, the Austrian scientist and philosopher Rudolf Steiner formulated special geometrical drawings or doodles for teaching purposes (one of these, which I have called the 'mystical crystal', is outlined at the end of this chapter). Steiner's drawings are still used all over the world in the Walddorf schools he founded. Children as well as adults find them intriguing and enjoyable as well as very effective in helping to improve self-assurance, organization skills, concentration and the ability to visualize in detail. In addition, the exercises develop a feeling for form, structure, harmony and rhythm.

Why is doodle therapy effective?

Doodle therapy works because the pathway established by the central nervous system between the brain and the hand producing the doodles is two-way. Normally it is thoughts and feelings in our subconscious mind which primarily influence the action and nature of our doodling. However, this influence can be reversed. By consciously choosing to draw certain therapeutic doodles we can use doodles to influence, in a positive way, our subconscious attitudes and emotions. This can significantly improve our psychological and physical sense of well-being.

When to do the exercises?

Choose one or more of the following exercises to do at a time when you feel they are relevant for the particular mood or state of mind you are in. If possible carry out the procedure twice a day. In order to give yourself a chance to obtain the most benefits from doodle therapy, regular practice is vital – the benefits are more than worth the small effort required. If you can do a session each night shortly before bedtime, this will help your subconscious mind to reinforce the effects subliminally whilst you are asleep.

Some helpful tips

Each exercise should be performed as smoothly and calmly as possible. Sit comfortably, with good posture, at a desk or table. Using a pen, pencil or felt-tip that feels good and a minimum of two pages for each doodle.

If you get tired, take a moment to stretch, close your eyes, or rest your doodling hand briefly. The aim is to stimulate your subconscious into producing the desired beneficial changes, and this works better if you are relaxed. Date and file each exercise so you can track your progress. Note down any changes in your state of mind or feelings at the end of each session. You will notice a considerable increase in the positive effects when you reach a fluency that enables accuracy with minimum effort.

How long will it take to experience the benefits?

The time required to gain the effects of the therapeutic doodles varies considerably from person to person. Some individuals have great difficulty in developing new physical skills or altering unwanted habit patterns, whereas others find it easy. Sometimes positive changes can occur very rapidly, but it might take weeks, or even longer, to notice significant improvements in deeply rooted aspects of personality and behaviour. In such cases, a daily practice of meditation is invaluable.

Doodle Therapy exercises

Melting anger/creating humour/ dissolving stress

Smiling faces

Any form of smiling face is appropriate, as long as the doodles have a smooth, rounded appearance, with no jaggedness or sharpness. *Think of anything that makes you feel happy and relaxed and keep this in mind whilst drawing your smiling faces.*

Flowing hearts

These should flow in smooth, continuous curved strokes. As you draw, focus some awareness on a person (or animal) who fills your heart with love.

The infinity chain

Choose a size for this doodle that feels good, and then, with smoothly flowing movement, aim to keep the upper and lower loops of this chain as round and consistent in length and width as possible, and equidistant. Leave plenty of space between each figure 8 as this increases the tranquilizing effects. Also allow enough space between rows to avoid entanglement – if you wish, use lined paper until you master a balanced and symmetrical construction of this doodle. Whilst doing this exercise, let your eyes gradually drift into a soft, lightly focused, effortless gaze. This exercise is designed to create a relaxed, harmonious, balanced state of mind – it can sometimes even relieve headaches.

Peaceful swans

The drawing of each swan should begin just above the beak, and continue in one harmonious flowing motion until the body and wings are completed. Only then should the pen be lifted in order to draw the beak and the eye of the swan. After a certain amount of practice you will find this drawing easy to do and highly enjoyable. Draw slowly and smoothly whilst visualizing a swan floating peacefully on a tranquil lake.

ENHANCING PHYSICAL CO-ORDINATION

COMBINED CURLS

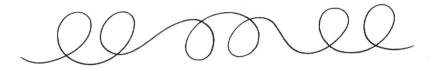

In this pattern you should aim for symmetry and fluidity – loops should be similar in size, and as smooth, round and flowing as possible. The distance between the upward- and downward-pointing pairs of loops should remain consistent throughout each row and the pen should move across the page in a continuous flowing movement maintaining an even tempo. When you do this exercise correctly and effortlessly it feels great.

PERFECT CIRCLES

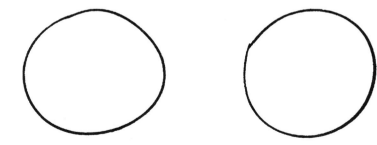

When drawing perfect circles, keep your spine erect and loose, with the pen upright, holding it as lightly as possible. Throughout the exercise maintain a constant background awareness of the sensation – or energy field – of your whole body. Hold the pen in front of you over the paper, waiting for the movement to begin. If you worry about how to move your hand, you will tense up. Just relax and sense the energy field in and around your whole body – the pool of energy that is the source of all creativity. Now draw an empty circle in space. Reverse it, and then make a figure of eight shape. See if you can maintain a sense of relaxation and flow throughout all the movements. Move the pen a little closer to the surface of the paper. Don't touch the paper yet; just enjoy looking at its blankness. When you feel ready to make the first stroke on the paper, let go of all speculation about the outcome. Just approach the paper without expectations. Let the first movement take over. Sense the connection between the pen and the paper. Is it a nice, flowing feeling or are you creating unnecessary friction with the tip of the pen? Observe this without any positive or negative judgement. Let nothing interfere with the energy flow of your movements, the smooth continuous path of your line. With practice you will enter a meditative state of mind, and when this happens the lines will connect precisely and your circles will become closer to perfect roundness.

IMPROVING MENTAL FOCUS AND MOTIVATION

Pointed domes

Where the domes connect, and also at the top of each dome the line should be retraced once or twice with maximum precision without taking the pen off the paper. Each dome should be upright and symmetrical so that the distance either side of the dotted line is almost identical. The height and width chosen for the first dome should be maintained closely throughout the exercise. If you need to, use graph paper until you master a balanced and symmetrical construction. Achieving excellent symmetry in this exercise will greatly help in balancing the activity in the right and left hemispheres of your brain. Your concentration and memory will become significantly sharper, and you will notice an improvement in your physical co-ordination and balance. When faced with a difficult project that you are dreading, successfully drawing a page of these pointed domes will help to get you started and increase your enthusiasm and efficiency.

Dissecting Lines

Lines should be of equal length and intersect precisely at the centre.

The Flowing Maze

This doodle is formed with one continuous unbroken line. The space between parallel lines should be as equal and even as possible. Learning to draw this pattern accurately requires, and develops, incredible mental focus and co-ordination.

The Mystical Crystal

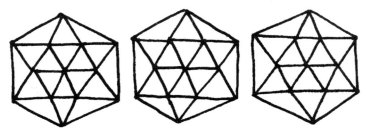

The aim of this exercise is to produce a highly proportional, balanced structure without any real effort (this will take some practice). One easy method to do this is to begin by drawing a hexagram (six-pointed star). If you succeed in drawing this proportionally, adding the remaining lines to complete the shape will not be too difficult. You can practice drawing this shape from different starting points – try beginning with the lines that cross at the centre of the shape. The full effects of this Rudolf Steiner exercise are described at the beginning of this chapter.

INDEX

abstract doodles 65–68
aerials 82
aeroplane 82
Ajna Chakra 22
alien abduction 82
almond 83
alphabet 83
analytical drawing psychology 3
anchor 83
angel 83
anima 44
animal doodles 69–78
ankh 64
ant 79
apple 83
arrows 39–40
Australian Aborigines 8

baby 83
baggage 83
ball and chain 83
ballerina 84
balloon 84
bambi 84
basket 84
bicycle 84
broom 85
brown 45
bubbles 85
bull 71
butterfly 80

cactus 86
cake 86
camel 71

candle 86
cannon 86
car 86
cartoon characters 87
cash 87
castle 37
cat 71
caterpillar 80
cell bars 87
cemetery 87
central nervous system 113
chain 87
chair 87
checkerboard 67
cheese 87
chessboard 67
children 87
cuddly toys 107
Cupid 89
curtain 89

daisy chain 89
Dali's doodle 89
dartboard 89
desk 89
devils 89
diagrams of subconscious 1
diamond shape 62
dice 90
Disney characters 90
dissecting lines 119
dog(s) 72
doll 90

Donald Duck 90
doodle therapy 113
dots 67
dove 70
dragon 72
drum 90
dynamite 90

eagle 70
ear 26
earrings 90
egg shape 62

frog 73
funnel 92
gallows 92
games 67
garbage 92
Garden of Eden 8
gargoyles 89
gate 92
geometric doodles 58–65
ghosts 93
giraffe 73
goat 73
golf club(s) 93
Goofy 93
grapes 93
graphological principles 4
grass 93
great tree 8
green 45
grey 45
guitar 93
gun 93

hair 27–28
halo 93
hammer 93
hand 94
handcuffs 94
hang-glider 94
horse 74
Hulk 106

ivy 95

jack-in-the-box 96
jar 96
jaw/chin 26
Jekll/Hyde 43, 52
jewellery 96
jug 96
Jung, Carl 2–4

key/key hole 96
kinaesthetic 15
kites 96
knot 96

ladder 96
ladybird 80
lamb 74
landscape doodles 96
leaves 96
light blue 44
light bulb 97
lighthouse 97
lightning 64
lilly/lotus 97
lines 53–55
lion 75
lizard 75
logical reasoning 41
logos 97

motorcycle 99
mythology 8

naked figure 100
names 100
neck 27
necktie 100
nest 100

non-doodler 6
noose 100
nose 23–24
noughts and crosses 67
nude drawings 30
number board 68
numbers 38

oasis 100
octagon 63
octopus 76
ornate objects 100
owl 70

padlock 100
parachute 101
paradise 8
peaceful swans 116
peeping tom 101
pen pressure 48
penguin 70
penises 32–33

red 44
religious imagery 102
repetitive patterns 56–57
retracing 51
ribbon 102
riding doodles 102
ring 102
river 102
robot 103
rocket 103
roller coaster 103
rolling pin 103
romantic doodles 42
rose 103
ruler 103

saxophone 103
scales 103
scorpion 80
screw 104
scribbles 66
scroll 104
sea 104

seashell 104
secondary characteristics 111
seesaw 104
sixth sense 41
spring 65
square 60
squiggles 66
squirrel 77
stairs 106
star(s) 63, 106
submarine 106
suitcase 106
sun 106
superhuman 106
swan 71
swirl 65
symbolic imagery 2, 4
syringe 106

table 107
tail 77
target 107
teardrop 107
teddy bears 107
teeth 24–25
telescope 107
tent/tepee 107
therapeutic doodles 112
third eye 22
three-domensional doodles 57–58

weapons 110
whale 78
wheels 110
whips 110
wings (animal/human) 110
witch 110
wizard 111
word doodles 111

zebra 79